CROWD IDOLS

David Clayton is the editor of *Manchester City Magazine*, the club's official publication. He writes for the *Manchester Evening News* and has contributed to *The Guardian*. He is also the author of *Everything Under the Blue Moon*, *The Little Book of Man City* and *Blue Blood*, and recently co-authored *Maine Man*, the autobiography of Manchester City legend Tony Book.

CROWD IDOLS

MANCHESTER CITY
HEROES 1966 – 2006

DAVID CLAYTON

MAINSTREAM
PUBLISHING
EDINBURGH AND LONDON

First published in Great Britain in 2006 by
MAINSTREAM PUBLISHING COMPANY
(EDINBURGH) LTD
7 Albany Street
Edinburgh EH1 3UG

ISBN 1 84596 057 2

All photos courtesy of the *Manchester Evening News*

A catalogue record for this book is available
from the British Library

Typeset in Hammer and Janson Text
Printed in Great Britain by
William Clowes Ltd, Beccles, Suffolk

For Bear
All my love, little bro' x

CONTENTS

ACKNOWLEDGEMENTS

There are a number of people I'd like to thank for helping me get this book onto the shelves. The first person is Bill Campbell at Mainstream Publishing. Bill is always open to ideas and is happy to let you get on with it once the initial pitch has been accepted, and it's much appreciated. Thanks too to Graeme Blaikie for his usual laid-back approach to deadlines and the understanding that we writers need flexible friends from time to time – some more than others. Also, a massive thank you to Wayne at MEN Syndication for a fantastic deal on the pictures I chose.

The club is always helpful and supportive – they've certainly helped me on every project I've ever been involved with, and, again, it's greatly appreciated. Also, thanks to all the players I've included in this book and hundreds of others I couldn't – collectively you have given me such happiness and ridiculous highs over the years, of course levelled by, at times, the depths of despair. If City were my girlfriend, we'd have split up and got together so many times I would have to have had a revolving door fitted to the front of my house.

Thanks also to the lads at the unofficial City site www. mcfcstats.co.uk, an invaluable source of facts – thanks lads! You saved me a large amount of time.

Many thanks as well to Nick Davis, my editor, for considered (and often far better) suggestions during revision. Nick knows his stuff about the Blues, and that, I believe, is the key to a damned good editor.

To the City fans who are – and I know I'm on safe ground here but, ah, to hell with it – just different class. As Sister Sledge so succinctly once put it, 'We are family' – and a bloody big family at that, but a close one, too – nuff said.

Last, but by no means least, my blood family. Rather than the usual Oscar speech, I thought I'd keep it brief, so a huge thanks to my wife Sarah ('Haven't you finished it *yet*?') and my wonderful children, Harry, Jaime and our new arrival Chrissie. Also, thanks to my mum for helping me with some of the players who were before my time ('Ooh, yes, the fans loved him!') and my dad, brother Rowan and nephews Paul and Steve for their various views en route to the City of Manchester Stadium. Lastly, I've dedicated the book to my sister Wendy – another lifelong Blue and a fantastic role model for any snotty-nosed kid to look up to. Plus I owe her one for pushing her into a hot bath once and almost confining her to a life of being a double for the Singing Detective. That's about it. Thanks to you, too, for buying it and see you at the match!

FOREWORD

As the saying goes, I can't define an elephant, but I know one when I see one. So it is with a 'Crowd Idol'.

Take two players of comparable skill, or two whose contributions are of equal value, or two whose interpretations of the laws of the game show a similar degree of flexibility, and one might acquire the title for ever, the other not as long as he lives. Some come and go, leaving as much impression, as the Chinese say, as your hands when you take them out of a bucket of water; others can still elicit a smile long after their playing days are over.

Take away the small number of players who, it is generally agreed, were not a good idea and you are left with the vast majority who automatically are approved of the moment they put on the shirt. And then some go on to achieve that special status.

It can be a single incident or a gradual process, the possession of sublime gifts or the optimisation of what I shall call limited ability. Whatever it is, the crowd make the decision. We just *know*.

It's interesting that when a player is so described, it is sometimes faint praise; there is the implication that he isn't actually very good at football. Very often it's true. Well, so what? It's what he brings to the occasion that matters.

And some of the game's more heated discussions take place when a manager decides to sell a Crowd Idol. Why is it that two factions can see things so differently? Because we're entitled to make that decision.

Whether it's talent, commitment, aggression, humour, arrogance or the prospect of a few fireworks, something makes the difference between a dutiful and considered round of applause and a big cheer and a grin.

As is normally pointed out at this point, the inclusion or exclusion of players in a work such as the one you're about to read is a matter of opinion, an opportunity for debate and a chance to examine your own criteria. What is not clear, in my view, is why there's no mention of Jamie Pollock.

James H. Reeve
Manchester, March 2006

INTRODUCTION

What exactly is a Crowd Idol? Is it someone that transcends the general humdrum of day-to-day football by lifting us a little higher with a moment of magic? Is it a player that scores fantastic goals from time to time or one that gets tap-ins on a regular basis? Or maybe it's the local boy made good who leads his team with his heart and is prepared to shed blood for the shirt. It could even be an individual who just gives his lot every time he goes out and plays.

A select few fit all the above descriptions but a large number slot into one or two of the categories and that is the basis of this book. *Crowd Idols: Manchester City Heroes 1966–2006* looks at the players who were loved by the City fans for one reason or another. In all honesty, it was a tough call choosing those who make up the Top 50.

There were at least a dozen who missed out who I had to think long and hard about but to coin a cliché, at the end of the day, it's all about opinions. If I'd selected players I thought were Crowd Idols purely based on whom I thought other people might choose, I don't think I could have seen this project through. Therefore, although the lion's share of the players included were undoubtedly idols to most City fans, I doubt another individual would share exactly the same 50.

I may have been watching City for almost 30 years, but I thought it only right to cover the stars of our glorious heritage and did the necessary research to discover who were the real crowd favourites before my time. I've watched endless videos and spoken to as many people from that era as possible, as well as reading books and newspaper reports of the day, to ensure I was on the right lines.

However, there are a number of players not included that might cause an eyebrow to be raised or even the comment 'Is he having a laugh?' to be uttered. There's no Alan Oakes, no Glyn Pardoe or Garry Flitcroft and no Andy Hinchcliffe. Ian Brightwell didn't make my Top 50 either, but in each case it's not because I don't think they were popular – I know that all of those five just mentioned were popular, but that alone is not enough, at least not in my book, which this sort of is. To me, it needs more than just respect and admiration – there has to be something else. Call it the X-factor or the title of some other duff TV show if you want, but there has to be something else.

In the case of one or two players, it was just one or two things they did, but with the majority, it was much more. I've no doubt you will agree with most of the players in the Top 50, but there will certainly be a few who you don't. Leaving Tommy Caton and Steve Redmond out wasn't easy, and you may compare them with some of the selections and completely disagree.

In each case, I've tried to explain why they are included and why I thought they were loved on the terraces, but we're all different, and one man's Gio Kinkladze is another man's Gerry Creaney. It's horses for courses (or in Gerry's case, carthorses, at least when he played for City – sorry, big man).

But as long as you enjoy reading about some of the greatest players to have played for City over the past 40 years and feel the money you spent on this book – be it £10 or 25p at a car boot sale – was money well spent, that'll do for me.

David Clayton
Manchester, March 2006

50–41

THE SQUAD MEMBERS

NO. 50: ROCK SOLID REID – NICKY REID

SIGNED: 1977 from Whitehall Juniors & 1982 from Seattle Sounders

LEFT: 1982 for Seattle Sounders & 1987 for Blackburn

CROWD IDOL RATING: *

NICKNAME: 'Reidy'

APPEARANCES: 256 (+6 as sub)

GOALS: 2

SPECIALITY: Heading, with the occasional dribble

GREAT GOAL: Late winner v. Shrewsbury Town 1984

UNFORGETTABLE MOMENT: The Kippax's sit-down protest at Reid's exclusion from the team in preference to Kevin Bond

FLAWS: Unsafe to be sat high in the stand when he shaped to shoot

Nicky's tale: It was a tough call to decide between Steve Redmond, Tommy Caton and Nicky Reid for the final slot in this Top 50. All three wore their heart on their sleeve and gave everything for City, and the remaining two would undoubtedly take up positions 51 and 52 if they were available. But they aren't and so Nicky Reid is the final choice; the fact he was born in Manchester means he just edges out two talented Merseysiders.

Reid could not have had a more dramatic or high-profile start to his career when he was pitched in against Borussia Mönchengladbach in the last eight of the 1978–79 UEFA Cup. Aged just 18, he found himself face to face with European Footballer of the Year Allan Simonsen but more than held his own in a 1–1 draw.

It had been Malcolm Allison who threw the youngster in at the deep end and Reid would be one of the manager's few successes during an appalling second spell at Maine Road.

Reid was not in the man-mountain mould of the traditional centre-half but rather more like the old-fashioned half-backs of a decade earlier. In fact, many compared him to a young Mike Doyle – high praise indeed – and he made his league debut a couple of weeks later in a 2–1 defeat at Ipswich Town, before filling in for the injured Ray Ranson for several games towards the end of the campaign.

Tough tackling and brave, Reid soon became a crowd favourite – his type invariably do – and he started 22 league games the following season. In 1980–81 he further established himself with thirty-seven league appearances as well as turning out in fourteen of the Blues' fifteen cup ties that campaign, two of which were at Wembley. In what proved to be a productive year, he also collected the first of six England Under-21 caps against Hungary.

The following year saw Reid at the heart of a major controversy that was no fault of his own. Despite his impressive displays, the local boy made good was dislodged from the back four when John Bond signed his son, Kevin, to partner Tommy Caton at the heart of the Blues' defence. Reid wasn't dropped but instead moved into midfield, where at times he seemed unsettled and distracted. The City fans saw Bond junior as the culprit and gave him something of a hard time, with even the odd chant of 'daddy's boy' audible at home games. It was unfair but, at the same time, understandable. Bond was booed for a period, and there was even a sit-down protest on the Kippax during one game by those in favour of Reid returning to his rightful role – a good 50 per cent of the Kippax as it transpired.

Whether the manager was right to do what he did is open to question, but the fact that Kevin seemed to win favour over local hero Reid just didn't sit well with the majority. By the end of the campaign, Reid had actually played three more league games than Bond.

Unable to reclaim his role in central defence, he left in May 1982 to try his luck in America, only to return a few months later to resume his City career, scoring two late goals in three games after failing to score in any of the previous five years' worth of matches. Bond left the next year, and Reid finally had his favourite position back and also a new partner in the form of Mick McCarthy. The pair formed a solid spine that helped win promotion for Billy McNeill, but Reid was played at right full-back during the following season with Kenny Clements having returned to Maine Road following a spell at Oldham.

Certain managers clearly had a problem with Reid at centre-back. He hardly played the next season and instead left for Blackburn Rovers on a free transfer, clocking up more than 170 games for the Ewood Park outfit. He did return to City for a while as a physio, and in February 2006, he moved to Bury in a similar capacity.

NO. 49: BIG MAC – BOBBY McDONALD

SIGNED: 1980 from Coventry City
LEFT: 1983 for Oxford United
CROWD IDOL RATING: *
NICKNAME: 'Bobby Mac'
APPEARANCES: 111 (+1 as sub)
GOALS: 16
MOMENT IN TIME: Celebrations after the final whistle v. Watford, 1982, after deputising in goal for Joe Corrigan and keeping a clean sheet during a 1–0 win
SPECIALITY: McDonald's drive-throughs – perfect timing when scoring from corners
NOT A LOT OF PEOPLE KNOW THAT: Bobby became a paramedic on an ambulance crew in Aberdeen after retiring from the game

Bobby's story: Bobby McDonald arrived with Tommy Hutchison from Coventry City to help revive the ailing Blues, under the stewardship of John Bond at that time. Gerry Gow completed the mythical 'Tartan Trio', and the three wily Scots helped transform City from useless to useful in a matter of weeks as Bond's side made a dramatic about-turn in league and cup form.

McDonald's role at left full-back was to provide experience for a back four that had seen a plethora of teenagers regularly put to the sword by various opponents in the early part of the campaign. He was a solid tackler, keen in the air and willing to put himself in the line of fire for his new club.

He was also one of the best attacking defenders of his day – a real threat from any set piece but especially corners. During the 1981–82 season, the Blues were perhaps the most difficult team to defend a corner against, and McDonald was the main reason.

The near-post flicks almost always caused havoc in the opposition's box, and McDonald had an uncanny knack of arriving right on cue, launching himself at any ball that was fair game and being almost impossible to mark, with the ball often ending up in the back of the net.

His contribution to the Blues' FA Cup run was crucial, and he scored several vital goals along the way to the 1981 Centenary final against Spurs. He bagged one in the 6–0 victory over Norwich and then scored two in two minutes in the quarter-final replay against Everton. Without McDonald that evening, City may never have progressed to the last four. By the end of the season, he'd amassed eight goals – not bad for a full-back!

In his second campaign with City, he added another six goals to his tally, though his compatriots Hutchison and Gow began to fade from the first-team picture as Bond reshaped the team using some of the money earned from the two Cup final matches against Spurs.

His third season at Maine Road was one of breathtaking contrast. Having won the first two games of the new campaign at Norwich and at home to Stoke, City took on a vibrant Watford for the chance to go top of the first published table. Almost 30,000 had gathered to inspire Bond's team to the summit, and with three minutes on the clock, Dennis Tueart scored to give the hosts a 1–0 lead. Minutes later and Joe Corrigan, City's keeper, was being helped from the pitch with a dislocated shoulder.

Only one sub was allowed in those days and nobody used a goalkeeper as the extra man. Step up Bobby Mac, almost swallowed by Big Joe's green jersey and gloves, to take his place in goal. He had more than 80 minutes to keep out a lively and dangerous Watford attack, but the defence held strong, and the whole team defended as though their lives depended on it – and when Watford finally did break through, McDonald kept out everything they could throw at him. It was an incredible display of resilience and bravery, and when the final whistle blew, the Kippax roared their approval in McDonald's direction, chanting his name for several minutes, their team now safely perched at the top of the table.

That was the last real high of McDonald's time with City, as the club then embarked on a woeful run of form that saw them relegated on the final day against Luton Town. McDonald moved on as Billy McNeill took over the reins at Maine Road and the last of the bargain buys John Bond had signed was gone. City fans, though, will always have a soft spot for the balding, dashing full-back with an eye for goal and, it has to be said, a knack of keeping the ball out of the net, too.

NO. 48: THE MEXICAN BANDIT –

MAURIZIO GAUDINO

SIGNED: 1994 on loan from Eintracht Frankfurt, £200,000
LEFT: 1995 (loan expired)
CROWD IDOL REATING: *
APPEARANCES: 21 (+4 as sub)
GOALS: 4
SPECIALITY: Milking crowd ovations
CATCHPHRASE: 'Can I borrow your car keys?'
GREAT GOAL: Stooping header v. Liverpool 1994
UNFORGETTABLE MOMENT: The way he ambled just long enough to be the last off the pitch after scoring the winner v. Liverpool
FLAWS: Wrong place, right time

Maurizio's story: Born in Germany, the roguishly good-looking midfielder Maurizio Gaudino added a touch of flair and invention to the Blues' midfield with his exotic array of flicks, tricks and individual skill. Gaudino arrived at City with a reputation of being something of a playboy. Aged 21, he raced around his local neighbourhood in a Ferrari which, alongside his shades, leather jacket and flowing black curly locks, didn't go down too well with the more reserved residents of Rheinau.

He played alongside Tony Yeboah and Uwe Bein at Eintracht Frankfurt and soon came to the notice of the German national team, being included in the World Cup squad for USA '94. But a disagreement with his club coach led to his refusal to play against SV Hamburg, and after a subsequent suspension, he soon found his way out to England on a loan deal with Manchester City. Free from the controversy and baggage he'd left back home, arriving with a clean slate to play for Brian Horton's side must have been like a breath of fresh air for Gaudino, who quickly settled into the side and soon formed a bond with the City fans who, of course, love nothing more than a touch of

Maurizio Gaudino – a brief but sparkling stay from the German midfielder

genius about their midfielders. He made his debut in a surprise Coca-Cola Cup win at Newcastle United just three days after signing on 21 December 1994. Gaudino scored his first goal against Notts County in an FA Cup replay in which Uwe Rösler scored the other four during a 5–1 win. He sometimes skipped and waved like a child would after a good performance, but there was a shock in store for the gifted midfielder when, on 16 April 1995, he was accused by Mannheim state prosecutors of participating in a gang fencing stolen goods and cars. The prosecutor emphasised at the time that Gaudino was to be considered innocent until proven guilty in a court of law. The gang was eventually apprehended, leading to a one-year suspended jail sentence for Gaudino and prompting the Blues' fans to compose this little ditty to the tune of 'O Sole Mio' (that's 'Just One Cornetto', in case you're wondering): 'Just one Gaudino, from Man City, he's got a passion, for your car keys, he steals, Lamborghinis, he is Gaudino, from Man City.' That is just a terrace chant and not a fact! Please put those lawsuits on the backburner again, gentlemen.

The accusations all added to the mystique and underlined Gaudino's life in the fast lane. Meanwhile, his on-pitch antics left the City fans demanding he be signed, but despite twenty games and three goals under his belt and a host of top-notch displays, the permanent deal never materialised as manager Brian Horton was sacked by the Blues. It left Gaudino in a state of limbo, and, eventually, he realised the deal was never going to happen as City's search for a new manager lasted much of the ensuing summer months. He eventually joined Mexican club America, and Georgi Kinkladze was brought in a few weeks before the start of the new season, placating the bemused supporters who wondered what might have been if Gaudino had been signed.

NO. 47: THE CUMBRIAN EXPRESS – PAUL SIMPSON

SIGNED: 1982 from Cumbria Boys
LEFT: 1988 for Oxford United
CROWD IDOL RATING: *
NICKNAME: 'Simmo'
APPEARANCES: 127 (+28 as sub)
GOALS: 24
SPECIALITY: Crossing
SONG: 'Simmo! Simmo! Simmo!'
GREAT GOAL: Beating the Charlton goalie to the ball for City's second goal in a minute as they won 5–1 to secure promotion
UNFORGETTABLE MOMENT: His debut v. Coventry (1982)

Simmo's tale: Paul Simpson celebrated his sixteenth birthday by signing a contract with City, and just four months later, he became one of the club's youngest ever debutants, making a stunning bow in a 3–2 win over Coventry City. John Bond played him twice more before sending him back to the youth and reserve sides to learn his trade.

In fact, with the Blues relegated in 1983, Bond long since gone and his successor John Benson leaving the club, Simpson was almost forgotten about amid all the drama and it was another two years before he played first-team football again, now at the ripe old age of eighteen.

The fans loved his raw enthusiasm and old-fashioned wing wizardry, and new boss Billy McNeill decided he might just be the catalyst his side needed for the final promotion push in 1984–85. He drafted his young charge in for the last nine games, and it was an inspired move. Simpson scored seven times in the run-in, and in the final game, which City needed to win to guarantee promotion, he was the man of the match.

Against Charlton, he had a hand in three goals and scored one himself in an epic 5–1 win to gain promotion. From then on the No. 11 shirt was his, and in a tough return to Division One, Simpson, still only nineteen, more than held his own, scoring three goals in the first five games. He ended with eight from thirty starts. He wasn't afraid of reputations and took on seasoned campaigners (who had probably started their careers while he was still in primary school) with a refreshing approach that endeared him to the City fans.

He played in 32 league games in 1986–87 but was forced to celebrate his 21st birthday that summer as a Division Two player again as the Blues slipped ignominiously out of the top flight, having been unable to buy anyone of real quality and battling on with a squad that just wasn't good enough. Mel Machin was the fifth – and ultimately final – manager Simpson served under, and he employed the (still young) winger as an out-and-out wide man, there to provide goals for others, which he did – and more besides. His performance in the incredible 10–1 win over Huddersfield was devastating, setting up several goals in possibly his finest hour for the club.

However, cash-strapped City were powerless to turn down a £200,000 bid from Oxford United just two games into the 1988–89 campaign, and Simmo's last appearance in a blue jersey was an awful 4–1 home defeat by Oldham Athletic. He left the ground to chants of 'Swales out! Swales out!', as the supporters turned their anger on the chairman, and he must have been glad to be on his way from the turmoil. At 22, he was almost a veteran in many fans' eyes, and it was easy to forget he was still no more than a kid.

He was an energetic and genuine old-fashioned out-and-out

winger – the sort the Kippax loved to watch as he received the ball, put his head down and headed for the goal line before whipping over an inviting cross. Disappointingly, he left the club on the verge of a notable landmark, having made 99 league starts.

After spending four years with Oxford, he later enjoyed great spells with Derby County and Wolves before moving into management with Rochdale. He guided them to a famous 2–0 FA Cup win over Gary McAllister's Coventry City in 2003, before moving on to his hometown club, Carlisle United. He guided them back from the Conference to league football and, it seems at the time of writing, straight up to Coca-Cola League One at the first attempt, too.

NO. 46: BLACK VELVET – CLIVE WILSON

SIGNED: 1979 from Moss Side Amateurs

LEFT: 1987 for Chelsea

CROWD IDOL RATING: *

NICKNAME: 'Jive'

APPEARANCES: 124 (+2 as sub)

GOALS: 11

SPECIALITY: Neat, clever passing

GREAT GOAL: Diving header against United at Old Trafford

UNFORGETTABLE MOMENT: When the *Manchester Evening News* broke the story he'd been sold and Paul Stewart had been bought with the cash

FLAWS: None obvious

Clive's tale: Clive Euclid Aklana Wilson was signed from the highly regarded local Manchester team Moss Side Amateurs in 1979. City had an excellent reputation for signing local youngsters, and with Maine Road smack in the middle of Moss Side, many of the talented kids were plucked from the predominantly black community. Alex Williams, Dave Bennett, Gary Bennett, Roger Palmer and Clive Wilson were the cream of the crop, and Wilson, with his superb technical ability, became a firm favourite on the Kippax in the early 1980s.

He impressed in the youth team and was a key member of the side that reached the 1978–79 FA Youth Cup final, which the Blues won 2–0 on aggregate over two legs against Millwall. He was then promoted to the reserves with other members of the team, such as Nicky Reid, Tommy Caton, Alex Williams and Steve Kinsey, also progressing to the second string.

Wilson had to wait until December 1981 to make his full

league debut. He replaced Bobby McDonald at left-back as the Blues took on Wolves at Maine Road and had a very satisfying match, playing his part in the 2-1 win that took City to the top of the league. He was out of the side for the next three months before replacing McDonald again, this time at Middlesbrough, and then he played in midfield at home to Liverpool.

Despite his cool head and silky skills, the trauma of the 1982–83 relegation season meant he wasn't used at all by City, who instead loaned him to Chester where he made 21 starts for the Sealand Road outfit. Following the resignation of John Bond and the sacking of John Benson, new boss Billy McNeill used him just 11 times during the 1983–84 Division Two campaign. It was a mystery why this talented young footballer was continually being overlooked, but things were about to change.

The next two seasons saw Wilson used 51 times, far more in midfield, and the City fans loved the way he played his football – he was easy on the eye, a real City player. He couldn't be ruffled, and for a lightly built lad, he was made of strong stuff. Even so, it wasn't until Jimmy Frizzell took over as manager that Wilson finally won a regular place in the side. He was an ever-present during the 1986–87 season, but after finally achieving his goal of winning his shirt on a permanent basis, cash-strapped City sold him to Chelsea for £250,000 to raise the money needed to buy Paul Stewart from Blackpool. An agreement was struck that allowed Wilson to remain at City for the final two months of the season as the Blues battled against relegation, ultimately in vain.

Wilson went on to enjoy a very successful career with Chelsea, QPR and Spurs before retiring with Cambridge United aged 38. Quiet, popular and unassuming, Clive Wilson was always afforded a warm welcome on his returns to Maine Road. It was just a pity a succession of managers failed to spot what a gem they had in their midst. He could have been a great asset during a very turbulent time for the club.

NO. 45: THE MIGHTY ALEX – ALEX WILLIAMS

SIGNED: 1978 from Manchester Boys
LEFT: 1987 for Port Vale
CROWD IDOL RATING: *
APPEARANCES: 125
GOALS: 0
FLAWS: 'Glass back' towards the end of his time with City

Alex's tale: Alex Williams, English football's first high-profile black goalkeeper, had the perfect temperament to make it at the top. Sadly, injury ravaged a promising career, and Williams eventually faded away from the game, playing for a time in Scotland for Queen's Park and later for Port Vale.

Born in Moss Side, a mere stone's throw from Maine Road, Williams signed for City in 1978 and had Joe Corrigan and Keith MacRae ahead of him in line for first-team football. Even after a decade of playing at the highest level, Corrigan showed no sign of slowing down and MacRae had already spent the best part of five years in the shadows, waiting patiently for the odd scrap of action.

Williams was young, had time on his side and knew that, if he was patient, his chance would surely come. The first glimmer of opportunity came when MacRae joined Portland Timbers in 1981, having made just seventy appearances in eight years at the club. Williams stepped up to be Corrigan's understudy, and he made his debut in a 2–1 home win against West Brom in March 1981. He then played in the second match of the 1981–82 season at Notts County but had to wait until the penultimate game of the season (3–1 defeat at home to Coventry) for his next taste of senior football. When Corrigan dislocated his shoulder three games into the next season, John Bond called upon the rookie Williams for his first proper run at first-team level – but despite half-a-dozen games, he was still awaiting his first clean sheet. City were struggling and were embroiled in a battle to avoid relegation by the spring of '83. Bond had resigned, and when Corrigan decided to sever his 17-year association with the Blues and try his hand in America, Williams became the undisputed No. 1.

It also meant that the youngster had the weight of City's scrap for survival placed firmly on his inexperienced shoulders. Quite why interim boss John Benson would allow Corrigan to go at such a critical point in the club's destiny is hard to fathom. Meanwhile, Williams was put into the eye of the storm and was helpless to stop Southampton winning 4–1 at The Dell – the Blues' sixth defeat in seven games.

It wasn't until his fifteenth game for City that Williams managed to keep his first clean sheet, during a 2–0 win at West Brom. In the next six matches he kept another two but was on the losing side four times, setting up a final-day do-or-die clash with Luton Town. If Williams could keep the Hatters out for 90 minutes, City would stay up – even a point would be good enough.

Unfortunately, with minutes remaining, Luton sub Raddy Antic sent a low drive through a crowded penalty area. The unsighted City keeper was powerless to prevent the ball hitting the back of the net, and the game was lost, costing the Blues their top-flight status for the first time since 1966.

There was nothing Williams could have done to prevent City's fall from grace, and the following campaign he proved what a talent he was, winning an army of admirers as he helped the Blues to fourth place in the old Second Division.

He played in all forty-two league games, keeping eleven clean sheets along the way and did better still the next season as City reclaimed top-flight status by finishing third. Williams was an ever-present again and kept a record 21 clean sheets (until Nick Weaver broke the record in 2000) – a magnificent effort that had the Blues support demanding that their No. 1 be considered for England.

But after just eight games of the 1985–86 season, Williams was injured and ruled out for the rest of the campaign with a back problem. What should have been his career platform turned into a nightmare, and he would never play for the Blues again, despite his best efforts, going out on loan to Queen's Park in Scotland for a short spell. In fact, he never fully recovered from his injury, and despite battling on for a while with annual strugglers Port Vale, he was forced to retire early. He returned to Maine Road as a community officer and today heads the highly innovative and respected 'City in the Community'. He won an MBE a couple of years ago and is still a hugely popular figure at the club today. What he might have achieved on the pitch had he not been so unfortunate will never be known, but international recognition would surely have come sooner or later, and, even now, he remains one of only a select few black keepers to have played at the highest level.

NO.44: RAGING BULL – PAUL STEWART

SIGNED: 1987 from Blackpool, £200,000

LEFT: 1988 for Tottenham, £1.7 million

CROWD IDOL RATING: *

NICKNAME: None

APPEARANCES: 63

GOALS: 30

SPECIALITY: Powering his way relentlessly forward

SONG: 'One Paul Stewart!'

GREAT GOAL: His hat-trick against Huddersfield during the 10–1 win

UNFORGETTABLE MOMENT: Brace at then leaders Bradford City in 1987

FLAWS: Worth too much to a team with no money

Stewart's tale: Paul Stewart's contribution to Manchester City should not be overlooked, though in the annals of time, it often is. He was at Maine Road for barely 15 months, but he instantly bonded with the fans and became a shining light who helped take the club forward – genuine Crowd Idol material.

Stewart was signed from Blackpool in March 1987 at a cost of £200,000 with the proceeds of Clive Wilson's move to Chelsea; both deals were announced on the same day, one delighting and one dismaying the supporters. With City, you used to have to lose a crowd favourite in order to gain one; at least that's how it was under Peter Swales.

Stewart was a Manchester lad who had been at Blackpool for six years and had managed fifty-six goals in one hundred and eighty-eight league starts. Physically powerful, quick and with some nice touches, the 23 year old was exactly what manager Jimmy Frizzell was looking for as he sought a forward who could perhaps help the Blues stave off relegation from the old First Division. The gamble failed and City, who, in truth, had appeared doomed anyway, slipped out of the top flight. Stewart only scored twice in those first eleven games as he tried to find his feet in a division two higher than he'd played for most of his career.

But if the top flight was out of his reach at that point, the Second Division was tailor made for him. He managed just one in his first five games of the 1987–88 season, but once he clicked into gear, he was an unstoppable force. The fans loved him. He was a local lad who had no airs or graces about him, and he came across as an almost old-fashioned centre-forward who took the knocks in his stride and was happy to get in amongst it if need be.

When City went to leaders Bradford in late October, the Bantams were unbeaten at home and leading the pack impressively. They were the team to chase, but City went to Valley Parade and comprehensively turned them over in a 4–2 win. Stewart was immense, scoring twice and generally terrifying the home defence every time he had the ball. Mel Machin had come in as manager during the summer and was mixing youth with experience in a team that just wanted to attack.

The defence wasn't so hot, but when the Blues racked up a 10–1 win over Huddersfield, the whole country sat up and took notice – as well as a host of scouts who began sniffing around the City forwards who were scoring almost at will at that point. Stewart, David White and Tony Adcock all scored a hat-trick against the Terriers in a unique and unforgettable day at Maine Road. The scouts went back to their employers with glowing reports of several of City's promising young stars but particularly Stewart, who was fast maturing into the best forward outside the top division.

At the end of the year, he had 17 goals from 26 league appearances. The explosive momentum from the opening four months of the 1987–88 campaign could not be sustained into 1988, and Stewart managed to score in just five of the next fourteen games. Had he been unsettled by constant media speculation about his future or even tapped up by this point? It's possible the media glare came too quickly for him to handle particularly well.

His profile was raised further by the Blues – whether they were playing in the Second Division or not – especially as they reached the last eight of both the FA and League Cup competitions. This gave the scouts a chance to assess Stewart against the formidable defences of Everton and Liverpool. Unfortunately, the two teams from Merseyside put an end to any Wembley dreams for Machin's side. Stewart had proved, however, that he could indeed ruffle the feathers of a few top-name defenders, and that was as good as ringing the cash register for chairman Peter Swales.

City finished the campaign in a disappointing ninth position, but were considered one of the favourites to return to the top division the following season. With little or no money available, Machin had to generate funds himself, and when Spurs tabled a hefty bid of £1.7 million for Stewart, City reluctantly accepted the offer. Machin had his transfer kitty, but the Kippax had lost another hero. However, the Blues went on to win promotion that year and the board and manager's decision was fully vindicated.

But what of Stewart? The promising young forward held his own at White Hart Lane, but by the time he moved on to Liverpool four years later, he'd become an odd hybrid of forward-turned-midfielder. He seemed to have it all and a glittering future ahead of him, and though he undoubtedly made a success of his career, those Blues fans that had seen him crank up a couple of gears in such a short space of time just couldn't understand why things seemed to stall for him after leaving the Blues.

His scoring ratio for City was almost one every two games; after that, he managed just fifty-four goals in three hundred and twelve games for seven other clubs – around one goal every six matches. We can only wonder what might have been had he stayed at Maine Road, but, for a time, he was up there with the very best of that era.

NO. 43: SMOOTH OPERATOR – DAVID ROCASTLE

SIGNED: 1993 from Leeds (exchange deal with David White)
LEFT: 1994 for Chelsea
CROWD IDOL RATING: *
NICKNAME: 'Rocky'
APPEARANCES: 23
GOALS: 2
SONG: 'Oh, Rocky, Rocky! Rocky, Rocky, Rocky, Rocky, Rocastle!'
UNFORGETTABLE MOMENT: His double drag-back that left two Ipswich Town players rooted to the spot while he ran on, crossed the ball in and set up a goal up for Carl Griffiths

Rocky's tale: The tale of David Rocastle is ultimately a tragic one. The former Arsenal and England midfielder arrived at Maine Road via a short stay with Leeds United. David White moved to Elland Road in December 1993 and Rocastle moved to City in a straight swap valued at £2 million, making his debut against Southampton in a 1–1 draw just before the New Year.

He was an instant hit with the fans, and his class was painfully apparent in a side that included the likes of (no offence lads) David Brightwell, Alan Kernaghan, Kare Ingebrigtsen, Alfons Groenendijk, Carl Shutt and Carl Griffiths. In fact, it was a City side seemingly headed for relegation, though they would muster enough points to ultimately delay that particular treat for a couple of years.

Rocastle shone like a beacon, and for anybody who has played for a pub team or Sunday League outfit where an ex-pro has made a cameo appearance, that's how he looked at times in a poor City side. Fans clung to him like a life raft on a sinking ship, and he didn't disappoint, although everybody knew it was to be a brief affair. It had to be. Even though Rocky was on his own personal career descent, he still had what it took and

David Rocastle — a classy midfield addition to City, though his stay was all too brief

against Ipswich produced one moment of Brazilian skill that won over any doubters in a second.

He continued to ooze class, even when he was having an off day, and the oft-heard comment around Maine Road was, 'Imagine if we'd have got him five years ago.' Rocky only played twenty-three games for City, and it's amazing he made such a big impact given that he was only with the club for eight months – but he did, and there was a great deal of disappointment when he was allowed to join Chelsea a few weeks before the 1994–95 season. He was undoubtedly one of the big-earners at Maine Road, but the truth was that Rocky was finding life away from Highbury difficult, and he looked a little lost at times in his post-Gunners career. His time with the Blues proved that, on his day, he was still one of the best English midfielders of his generation.

Things didn't work out for him at Chelsea, either, and he went on loan to Norwich and Hull while at Stamford Bridge. He even tried his hand in Malaysia, but it was a mere stoking of the dying embers of a top-class career. Winning league titles and a host of trophies one minute and fighting relegation the next had not been the swan song he must have hoped for.

Then, in February 2001, it was announced that he was suffering from non-Hodgkin's lymphoma, and just two months later, he passed away. Rocky left behind a wife and three children, and though his time as a City player was short, he left a lasting impression on the pitch, as well as off it, where he proved equally popular. Respected and missed by those who knew him.

NO. 42: A CLASS ACT – TREVOR FRANCIS

SIGNED: 1981 from Nottingham Forest, £1 million
LEFT: 1982 for Sampdoria, £1 million
CROWD IDOL RATING: *
NICKNAME: 'Trev' (!)
APPEARANCES: 29
GOALS: 14
SPECIALITY: Speed and razor-sharp brain
SONG: 'One Trevor Francis!' or his personal theme 'Should I Stay Or Should I Go?'
CATCHPHRASE: 'Second-class dicket to Dottingham' – he had nasal issues
GREAT GOAL: 50-yarder v. Brighton in February 1982
UNFORGETTABLE MOMENT: Hitting two on his debut at Stoke
FLAWS: Utterly injury prone

Trev's tale: When Trevor Francis finally signed for City from Nottingham Forest in September 1981, the news was greeted with feverish enthusiasm by the fans. The ensuing scramble for tickets was not hampered by Stoke, who, with cash signs in their eyes, told the Blues'49 followers they could bring as many as they could pack in.

More than 10,000 travelled to the Victoria Ground to see Francis make his bow – and he didn't disappoint. The England forward was regarded as one of the best of his generation, and he wasn't over the hill or badly out of form like some of the strikers signed around that time. For Blues fans everywhere, it meant everything that he had chosen our club.

It demonstrated that the board believed, following the FA Cup final defeat to Tottenham just a few months earlier, there was a real chance that John Bond could guide the team to even greater heights – maybe even the league title.

Francis must have been a little bemused when he saw the masses of City fans banked behind the goal at Stoke, and he rewarded them with two goals in a stunning debut. City won 3–1, and the focus then shifted to Francis's home debut against Southampton a week later. A crowd of 42,003 crammed into Maine Road to watch a 1–1 draw and maintain the Blues' unbeaten start to the season, with Francis hysteria continuing unabated.

But just four games into his City career, he was ruled out for six matches with injury and the Blues failed to score in four of those games, winning just once. This was the precedent for things to come.

City then built up a head of steam, inspired by Francis, who seemed, at times, to be on another level. Dennis Tueart and Kevin Reeves were in fine form and benefiting from Francis's clever link play, and things were going well, even when Tueart was ruled out with injury for the rest of the season – this after scoring nine goals in fifteen games.

Francis was inspirational, a fantastic talent who lifted the crowd every time he had the ball. He was quick with an eye for the unusual and the rest of the team were all chipping in, but when City travelled to Liverpool on Boxing Day 1981, everyone expected the traditional mauling – City had lost fourteen and drawn one of their last fifteen visits and hadn't left Anfield with maximum points since 1953.

However, this City team had Trevor Francis leading the line, and the Blues raced to a memorable 3–1 win – a belated but most welcome Christmas present. Two days later, Wolves were put to the sword in a thrilling 2–1 win at Maine Road, and City ended the year as leaders of the First Division. It looked like Peter Swales's decision to sanction Francis's signing had been inspired, because if City could stuff Liverpool in their own backyard, why should they fear anyone?

But the New Year brought more injury woe for the Blues, and though the team's form was good up to mid-February, the loss of Francis for several games (he played eight and missed eight from the end of February to May) plus the loss of Tueart and Hutchison to long-term injury was too much for the side to sustain, and City finished the season in tenth position. Incidentally, Liverpool visited Maine Road in April to restore sanity by winning 5–0 – that taught us to mess with unsuccessful sequences!

By that point, Francis had become an expensive luxury. He looked unhappy and was continually injured, playing a couple of games here and there, and the momentum was lost. Swales decided he wanted his money back, and shortly after the season ended, Francis jetted off to Italy to join Sampdoria, for around the same fee he'd cost the club ten months before.

He left us with some wonderful memories and, for a while, allowed us to dream of the league title again. He was the football equivalent of a Porsche 911, and he cruised like a Rolls. He was a superstar again when he came to City and scored 14 goals in 29 appearances. He won ten England caps while at Maine Road, and it was nice to know that 'our Trev' was leading the line with the likes of Kevin Keegan, no less, for the Three Lions. Was he worth the money? Of course he was – every penny, and although it was merely a cameo, it was very sweet while it lasted.

NO. 41 THE INDOMITABLE LION – MARC-VIVIEN FOÉ

SIGNED: 2002 on loan from Lyon, £500,000
LEFT: 2003 for Lyon (loan expiry)
CROWD IDOL RATING: *
NICKNAME: 'Marco'
APPEARANCES: 38
GOALS: 9
MOMENT IN TIME: Scoring the last ever City goal at Maine Road
SPECIALITY: Midfield anchorman and 'spoiler'

Marc's story: Tragedy is an overused word in football, but the sudden death of Marc-Vivien Foé while playing for Cameroon in the Confederations Cup on 26 June 2003 was most definitely a tragedy. The tall holding midfielder joined City on loan in July 2002, and despite a bit of a shaky start, he soon settled into the team. He did the 'dirty stuff' as Stuart Pearce might say, breaking up play, winning headers, block tackling, marking, tracking and generally being a nuisance to the opposition.

In fact, it's fair to say that he took a while to win over the more sceptical City supporters at Maine Road, but by the end of the season, most fans respected his role in the side and recognised his importance to the team. He weighed in with nine goals too, no mean feat for a defensive midfielder. Sure, his touch was sometimes not the best, but that wasn't what Kevin Keegan had bought him for. He needed him as a spoiler, and, in retrospect, he was one of the best in the game at that job. He did the 'Patrick Vieira' role for the Blues, and it was only the following season that his worth was truly realised, although by then it was, sadly, too late.

He was born in Nkolo, Cameroon, and went on to play for

Lens, West Ham United and Lyon before joining the Blues on a season-long loan. He won 65 caps for his country and at just 28 years of age, arguably had his best years ahead.

Marc-Vivien Foé – did the jobs nobody else wanted to with great effect – much missed

He wasn't actually a City player when he ran out on that fateful day in Paris against Colombia. His loan had expired and Keegan was desperately trying to raise funds to bring him to Maine Road permanently. Lyon were happy to do business, and a fee of around £2 million would probably have secured his signature. Foé, it was later claimed, was happy to move to Manchester, and it all seemed a matter of when rather than if. Then, in front of millions of TV viewers, Marco collapsed on the pitch. He'd suffered a massive heart attack and died within seconds. It was an awful, horrible moment that nobody who witnessed it will ever forget, no matter how hard they try. The football world was in shock, and within hours of his death, flowers and football shirts were laid out at Maine Road as a mark of respect by the fans.

Within a few days, Maine Road's main entrance had become a shrine, with thousands of fans leaving all manner of tributes. The majority were from City supporters, but there were shirts and messages from fans of most British clubs. It was a moving and touching sight and one that meant so much to his young family.

Marco's last game for City had been on the final day of football at Maine Road – a game City lost 1–0 to Southampton. Pictures of the aftermatch lap of honour show a happy, smiling Marco – a sight those at the Blues' Carrington training ground saw on a daily basis. He was a very popular man behind the scenes, and he will forever be etched into the club's history books, having scored the last City goal at Maine Road in a 3–0 win over Sunderland. It is a fitting epitaph for a man many of us only came to appreciate once he'd been taken away, and his place in the Crowd Idols list is fully merited, even though it is for different reasons than the majority of other entries.

40–31

UTILITY PLAYERS

NO. 40: THE SILKY SCOT – TOMMY HUTCHISON

SIGNED: 1980 from Coventry City, £47,000

LEFT: 1982 for Bulova, Hong Kong (free)

CROWD IDOL RATING: * *

NICKNAME: 'Hutch'

APPEARANCES: 57 (+3 as sub)

GOALS: 5

SPECIALITY: Torturing hapless full-backs

CATCHPHRASE: 'Look into the eyes, not around the eyes, but in the eyes, and one, two, three, I'm past you.'

GREAT GOAL: Acrobatic header v. Spurs in the 1981 FA Cup final

UNFORGETTABLE MOMENT: Crestfallen on the Wembley turf after repeating the above goal, this time past Joe Corrigan in the same game

FLAWS: Advancing years

Tommy's tale: Tommy Hutchison was a football genius – no more, no less. He was a class act, and he should have gone down in history as a member of the select Wembley Winning Goals Club, but more of that later.

John Bond signed Hutch for peanuts from Coventry City, along with Bobby McDonald. Around the same time, Gerry Gow was also acquired, and never have three signings galvanised a side in quite the way that these three veteran Scots did. While McDonald was brutish effort and endeavour and Gow was gnashing teeth, bloodthirsty tackles and gnarled nous, Hutch was the ballet star, aesthetically beautiful to watch and full of grace. He was most definitely Friday's child.

The effect these three players had is well documented, but while it was easier to understand that McDonald and Gow had forged semi-successful careers making the most of what they had, Hutchison was something of a mystery. The first thing most City fans wondered when Hutchison made his home debut against Norwich was, 'How come we've never heard or seen much of this guy before?'

Tommy Hutchison – grace, guile and vision – a gem of a player

In the days before Sky TV, there were a number of players that you only occasionally saw on *Match of the Day* or read about. For many kids, you learned about the majority of players via the bubblegum football cards. Yet, aged 33, Hutch was no spring chicken when he joined City, so where had he been hiding all those years? Well, the answer to that seems to be the sleepy backwaters of Highfield Road, home of Coventry City. He spent eight years there, winning seventeen caps for Scotland, but the other Sky Blues were very much a low-profile club with little major exposure or success.

Hutch was voted Coventry's favourite player of the old First Division era in a recent poll, but it is still a mystery why he wasn't snapped up by a top club sooner – until City came in, of course. Hutch had something you can't teach kids – an ability to seemingly have all the time in the world every time he got the ball. There was rarely a wasted pass from a man whose physical appearance wouldn't have looked out of place in the Wild West, maybe as the hero sheriff who refuses to bow to the Gow Gang or whisky-guzzlin' cow rustlers . . . sorry, where were we?

He had an innate talent to look graceful in possession and seemed to glide with the ball rather than run. He was hardy, too, for a winger, but, then again, he was Scottish and was raised in Fife in the early 1950s where men were made of granite and women worked on oil rigs.

He fitted into John Bond's team like a glove, and City were soon climbing the league and on their way to an unforgettable FA Cup run. The City fans loved Hutch – he was an archetypal Manchester City player who played his part in saving the Blues from almost certain relegation during that first unforgettable season and started every cup tie on the road to Wembley. The cup final was a fitting *coup de grâce* for this most elegant purveyor of the game, and when fairy-tale-land beckoned with a spectacular goal against Spurs, few who knew him begrudged him a well-earned moment in the spotlight. Yet what happened later in that same game is now the stuff of legend. With the match entering the final ten minutes or so, Hutch, desperate to keep out a Spurs free-kick, peeled slightly to the left of a defensive wall as he'd heard Glenn Hoddle indicate he was going to bend it around the right-hand side of the wall. His decision resulted in him being just close enough to connect with the well-struck ball and totally redirect its flight past Joe Corrigan and into his own net.

He sunk to his knees for a moment or two, trying to absorb the moment and its implications: Spurs 1, City 1 with time still to play. However, both teams were dead on their feet, and there were no more goals. A replay was arranged for the following Thursday. Hutch still managed to provide the cushioned header that set up Steve Mackenzie's wonderful volley to make the score 1–1 in that game, but despite leading 2–1 at one stage, the Blues lost 3–2 thanks to two late goals. It was a miserable day. The City fans didn't forgive Hutch because there was no forgiving to do – it wasn't his fault and nobody (bar perhaps himself) held him responsible for the eventual outcome.

He came back for another season and, for a while, helped the club to top the table and go into the New Year as leaders. But he was injured in the 2–1 defeat at Southampton a week into 1982, and he never played for City again. He'd begun his time with the club with a 2–1 win over Brighton on the south coast and he'd ended it a few miles away at The Dell. Without him, City won just four times in eighteen games and plummeted from pole position to tenth. On 1 July, Hutch moved to Hong Kong club Bulova (don't ask!) and then headed off to Seattle Sounders for a while. Later, he became Swansea's manager for a short time and is in the Swans' record books as the oldest player ever to turn out at forty-three years, five months and nineteen days old. His role in City's recent history will not be forgotten.

NO. 39: NORTH POLE – KAZIU DEYNA

SIGNED: 1978 from Legia Warsaw

LEFT: 1981 for San Diego

CROWD IDOL RATING: * *

NICKNAME: 'Kazi'

APPEARANCES: 38 (+5 as sub)

GOALS: 13

SPECIALITY: Free-kicks

CATCHPHRASE: 'Where's the nearest Polish club?'

GREAT GOAL: Stunning volley away to Borussia Mönchengladbach, 1979

UNFORGETTABLE MOMENT: Scorer of first truly world-class free-kick v. Aston Villa, 1979

FLAWS: Feigning injury – for training!

Kaziu's tale: There was a tremendous build-up of expectation and excitement when City announced that Kaziu Deyna would be signing for Manchester City after the World Cup. This was a man revered as a hero in his homeland, and he had more than 100 caps for Poland. He'd captained his country during one of the most spectacular World Cup final tournaments ever in Argentina '78, and now the Blues were about to sign their first true European superstar – what could possibly go wrong?

Well, the answer to that is fairly straightforward. This is Manchester City we are dealing with here, and plenty could go wrong . . . and did.

It wasn't so much that there was red tape to cut through to bring Deyna to City, it was more like red cables. Deyna was a captain in the Polish Army, and City had to first secure his release from military service, then secure a deal with his club,

Legia Warsaw. The clubs agreed a fee of around £100,000, but the Polish side didn't want the cash as such, they wanted hardware: photocopiers, printers and the like. It was bizarre, to say the least, but City went along with their requests.

Kaziu Deyna – promised so much but delivered so little – yet still revered

The deal dragged on and on and on, and it wasn't until November that the graceful Pole finally signed for City, but this was just the start of what was to be a largely disastrous stay in Manchester. Deyna was hardly match fit when he arrived, and it was a further fortnight before he made his league debut at home to Ipswich Town. His appearance added around 6,000 to the Maine Road gate for a game which City lost 2–1, but at least the small contribution he made proved enough to convince the fans that he was indeed worth the wait.

Deyna missed the following game, and during the next match – another 2–1 defeat, this time at QPR – he picked up an injury that ruled him out of the next four games. He returned for another home defeat (3–2 to Chelsea – Kaziu was never going to have the problem of being tagged a talisman!) and was relegated to the bench for the 3–0 win at Spurs. It wasn't until the final eight games of the campaign that he returned to the side fully fit and made something of an impact.

His late stooping header against Middlesbrough was his first goal, and by the end of the campaign, he'd bagged six goals in just four home appearances. Against Aston Villa in the final match of the season, he bent a free-kick over the wall into the top corner of the net and received a rapturous ovation from the Maine Road crowd, who had, quite frankly, never seen the like before.

Deyna had the ability to always seem to have time on the ball, and he had a grace and poise all too rarely seen on these shores. The fans loved him, especially the youngsters, because he was an exotic luxury from foreign fields, an unknown quantity capable of beautiful football. They wondered what he would have in store for his first full season with the Blues. The answer was more stop-start runs in the side, more flashes of brilliance and more long absences because of injury.

When he did get into his stride, he scored goals and also made them for teammates. His volley against Borussia Mönchengladbach in the second leg of City's UEFA Cup quarter-final was proof that he had the ability to score against anybody, but there were huge question marks about his commitment to City. Tony Book would sometimes have to send people to the Polish Club that Deyna used to frequent when he should have been at Platt Lane, and for Book, there was one too many occasions that he picked up a mystery injury prior to training.

He was undoubtedly homesick at times and wanted to be near his own people, but whether he believed in his heart of hearts that joining City was a fair move for the club or himself was a different matter altogether.

Book and Malcolm Allison were sacked in 1980, and John Bond took over. After assessing the situation, Bond shipped Deyna out of Maine Road and off to North America, where he joined the San José Earthquakes. He appeared, briefly, in the 1981 movie *Escape to Victory* alongside the likes of Pelé, Sylvester Stallone, Michael Caine, Bobby Moore and former City idol Mike Summerbee.

When he played, the fans loved him, but frustrating would be the best way of describing Deyna's time with City. He didn't have the desire to cut it in England, even if he had the ability – the pace and aggression didn't suit his style of play. But his stay with the Blues left a few happy memories, and there was no doubting that he was a world-class talent. He is still adored in his homeland as one of Poland's greatest ever stars, even today, and loved by the youngsters who perched themselves on the Kippax wall during the late '70s.

Sadly, he died in a car crash on 1 September 1989 in San Diego, California. He was only 42 years old.

NO. 38: LE SULK – NICOLAS ANELKA

SIGNED: 2002 from Paris St-Germain, £13 million

LEFT: 2005 for Fenerbahçe, £7 million

CROWD IDOL RATING: * *

NICKNAME: 'Nico'

APPEARANCES: 101 (+2 sub)

GOALS: 45

GREAT GOAL: Solo effort in 3–1 win at Maine Road v. Everton, 2002

SPECIALITY: Penalties

UNFORGETTABLE MOMENT: Hat-trick at home to Aston Villa, 2003
 – including two penalties!

FLAWS: Didn't realise that he'd finally found his home/one-on-ones

Nico's tale: City sent out a message to the rest of the Premiership when Kevin Keegan secured the signature of Nicolas Anelka for the start of the 2002–03 season at a cost of £13 million. The French superstar, along with Sylvain Distin, represented a bold move by the Blues to ensure Premiership football would be played when the club moved to its swanky multi-million-pound stadium the following year.

Anelka arrived with plenty of baggage, and although a Paris Saint-Germain player, he'd spent the past five months on loan at Liverpool, where it was assumed he would move permanently. But when Gérard Houllier opted not to take the option of a permanent deal on Anelka, Keegan moved in with a cash bid that Paris accepted. After eggshell negotiations were completed with Anelka's representatives, he agreed to join City . . . and one of the biggest names in European football made his way to Maine Road.

He made his debut away to Leeds United, and despite a 3–0

defeat, Anelka's quality was there for all to see. He had speed, grace and a fluidity that set him apart from other strikers at the club.

He didn't find the net in any of his first three games for his new club, but he scored twice against Everton and was cruelly denied a hat-trick by the dubious goals panel, having destroyed the Toffees almost single-handedly. He scored in his next two games to make

Nicolas Anelka – sulky, yes, but on his day a treat to watch

it four from seven – a fair return from the club's record buy. City have had a number of great strikers over the years, and Anelka was up there with the best of them – a smooth-running Porsche engine beneath his jersey, he positively oozed class when he was in the right frame of mind. And while some of the more mature Blues might have reserved judgement on the man with a worse reputation for sulking than Worzel Gummidge, he was a god to the young supporters, hence his inclusion as a Crowd Idol.

With Eyal Berkovic and Ali Benarbia sending him clean through on numerous occasions – though he seemed to have an inferiority complex at one-on-ones with the keeper – Anelka struck up an unlikely partnership with Shaun Goater and the pair were at the heart of a stunning final Maine Road derby win over United. That game is best remembered for The Goat's efforts and for Gary Neville's inadequacies, although it shouldn't be forgotten that Anelka also wreaked havoc that afternoon.

City held their own that season, but Anelka, more used to the bright lights of London, Paris and Madrid, must have left the Maine Road pitch with a heavy heart when former clubs Arsenal and Liverpool crushed the Blues 5–1 and 3–0 respectively. At least Nico had the last laugh with his double strike earning a rare 2–1 success for City at Anfield later on in his first season with the Blues, which also denied the Reds a Champions League spot. Revenge was sweet, and he also ensured that he finished the season as the club's top scorer.

Better news was to come when City were awarded the final UEFA Cup spot via the Fair Play League for being the top-placed eligible club in the Premiership after a respectable ninth-position finish. It also meant Nico would be involved in European competition again, something he clearly craved.

Six goals in the first six games of the new season sent Anelka's popularity soaring to new heights as City settled into their new ground, and he was in double figures after the 6–2 trouncing of Bolton at the City of Manchester Stadium. But with Goater gone and Robbie Fowler failing to gel with him up front, Nico relied more and more on the wonderful talents of Shaun Wright-Phillips. Jon Macken was another who didn't link well with the Parisian, and although Paulo Wanchope did, he missed many games through injury.

Anelka began the New Year in sizzling form – seven goals in seven games – and ended the campaign as top scorer again with a magnificent haul of twenty-four strikes. Even the most cynical of Blues had to admit that Nicolas Anelka in full flow, untroubled and focused, was a treat to watch. And how the City fans stood by him in return, chanting his name, applauding his every move and even forgiving those numerous one-on-one situations he missed and his incredible ability to be caught offside time and time again.

There were games when he clearly wasn't motivated, and rumours spread that he'd had a fall-out with Keegan. French football magazine articles quoted him criticising the team and the club's ambition, though these were vehemently denied as 'poorly translated' comments. Hmm . . . it happened at least a half-dozen times.

With two years of his deal with City left, he began the 2004–05 season in style, scoring five in the first six games, and it was his penalty that gave Chelsea their only defeat of the season as they powered towards the Premiership title. But the rumours of an imminent departure sprang up prior to the 2005 January transfer window, and after a 2–1 New Year's Day win over Southampton, Anelka finally left City in search of Champions League football with . . . Fenerbahçe! Yes, those perennial Turkish kings of Europe were the new lucky owners of one (slightly flawed with plenty of excess baggage) classy centre-forward who proved that, ultimately, more affection and adoration than he'd had at any of his previous clubs didn't matter a jot in his quest for personal glory. He seems to have an insatiable wanderlust that makes it doubtful he'll ever find somewhere he is truly happy, and more's the pity, because he has plenty to offer. The fact is, though, he was idolised by many while he was a City player and therefore deserves his place in the Crowd Idols Top 50.

NO. 37 – THE IRISH ROVER: JOHNNY CROSSAN

SIGNED: 1965 from Sunderland, £40,000

LEFT: 1967 for Middlesbrough, £30,000

CROWD IDOL RATING: * *

APPEARANCES: 110

GOALS: 28

GREAT GOAL: Classic Crossan strike during friendly with Dinamo Moscow, December 1965

UNFORGETTABLE MOMENT: Exacting revenge on John Charles – twice his size – when City played Cardiff in 1965

Johnny's tale: When the Football League gave Northern Ireland international Johnny Crossan a life ban from British football after problems over a transfer from Coleraine to Bristol City, they couldn't have known that they were actually doing the immensely talented inside-right a massive favour.

The Londonderry-born Crossan was forced to seek employment on the Continent in order to continue his career and was one of the few British players who played in Europe during the mid-'60s. He signed for Dutch club Sparta Rotterdam and adapted to the European style of football that involved more technique and intelligence, which actually suited his game. He honed his not inconsiderable skills to such a standard that Belgian champions Standard Liège bought him to bolster their European Cup bid.

He earned rave reviews for Liège when they played in the competition and when the ban was lifted in 1962, he moved back to the UK with Sunderland, who paid £27,000 for his services. He became a Roker Park favourite in the process after scoring 22 league goals and helping them win promotion to Division One.

In January 1965, George Poyser brought the 27 year old to Maine Road for £40,000 to add a bit of invention to his ailing side, and he made his debut in a 2–0 home defeat to Derby County.

City finished eleventh in the Second Division that year with Crossan making sixteen league appearances and scoring three goals. The silky-skilled Irishman was then installed as captain by new manager Joe Mercer, and, largely inspired by the cunning and vision of Crossan, who played 49 times and scored an impressive 16 goals, City raced to the championship and promotion back to the First Division.

John Crossan – a Continental talent
from Northern Ireland!

A hugely popular player, Crossan's humour and relaxed attitude undoubtedly helped form the famous team spirit that would help City sweep all in their path within a few short years. Despite not being the most physically imposing of players, he could mix it with the best of them, and when a teammate was scythed down by the legendary Welsh man-mountain John Charles at Cardiff in March 1965, it was Crossan who returned the compliment – and then some! Nobody pushed Crossan around, and he'd stand up for anyone who he thought wouldn't do it for themselves, further endearing him to the City public.

The embryonic Mercer side was starting to take shape and suddenly the Blues had a plethora of talented flair players including Colin Bell, Mike Summerbee and Neil Young to choose from.

Crossan needed to be at his best for the tougher demands of the top flight but a pre-season car crash resulted in a knee injury that Crossan tried, foolishly, to cover up. He also had a grumbling appendix which was affecting his form. His decision to carry on playing backfired, and, at times, it seemed to some sections of the City fans that he wasn't giving his all for the club. The reason was, of course, he was incapable of performing to his usual standards because of his various ailments.

He was dropped for the visit of Manchester United in 1967 after a series of below-par displays had resulted in some City fans jeering him. Crossan, philosophical as ever said, 'I heard the jeers, but that's football. You are king one day, a peasant the next!' It was the beginning of the end of his City career, though he was reinstated for the remainder of the season.

Despite City holding their own during the 1966–67 campaign, Crossan's place was no longer guaranteed. He still played thirty-five times and scored nine goals for the Blues, but with the signing of Tony Coleman, who played a similar role to the Irishman, his days at Maine Road were clearly numbered.

In August 1967, his mesmeric skills made their way to Middlesbrough for £30,000, where he eventually finished his career. Johnny Crossan played twenty-four times for his country and earned ten caps whilst at Maine Road. A favourite amongst old and young alike, he was undoubtedly ahead of his time in terms of his technical skill.

NO. 36: HERE, THERE AND EVERYWHERE – TOMMY BOOTH

SIGNED: 1965 from Middleton Boys

LEFT: 1981 for Preston North End, £30,000

CROWD IDOL RATING: * *

NICKNAME: 'Boothy'

APPEARANCES: 487 (+4 as sub)

GOALS: 36

MISTAKES: A mid-seventies perm and moustache

SONG: 'He's here, he's there, he's every ****** where, Tommy Booth! Tommy Booth!'

GREAT GOAL: Last-minute winner in the 1969 FA Cup semi-final

Tommy's tale: Tommy Booth wasn't a Crowd Idol *per se*, but he was a great crowd favourite over a sustained number of years – 16 to be exact – and therefore deserves inclusion in this particular collection of Blue heroes. He wasn't a Kinkladze, Bell or Summerbee, nor was he a Doyle or a Hartford but the City fans will always have a place in their heart for Tommy and players of his ilk.

It's not just a loyalty issue that makes a player a Crowd Idol, at least in this writer's opinion. Otherwise there would be a dozen other names included in this book. There are so many other factors and Booth just about ticks all the right boxes. The Manchester-born centre-half first came to prominence when he took George Heslop's No. 5 shirt for the first time in October 1968. City's rearguard had not been at its best as the Blues attempted to defend their crown in rather lacklustre fashion.

One win in the opening nine games was not the form of

champions, but the young Booth performed admirably on his debut, and Joe Mercer opted to play him alongside Doyle and the ever-dependable Alan Oakes.

However, Booth really came to the fore in the last minute of the dramatic FA Cup semi-final with Everton when he stabbed the ball home to send the Blues to Wembley, where they beat Leicester City. He played in the final, too, meaning he hadn't missed a game along the way and had been part of a defence that had only conceded one goal in seven games.

In fact, Booth would become something of a talisman for City, appearing in both 1970 cup finals (League and European Cup-Winners' Cup) as well as missing just one league game all season. For the next five years, the No. 5 shirt was pretty much his, but when Dave Watson was signed from Sunderland in time for the 1975–76 campaign, it was Booth who had to step aside – unthinkable a year or so before.

But when Colin Bell was injured against Manchester United in the League Cup at Maine Road, manager Tony Book had no hesitation in turning to the versatile Booth to fill in Bell's midfield slot, and he responded with his best-ever goals tally – six – and was in midfield as City beat Newcastle to lift the 1976 League Cup.

He did revert to centre-half towards the end of the season when Watson suffered a back injury. His chances were limited the following year, although he did step in for the final eleven games, following Mike Doyle's early end to the campaign as City finished second in the old Division One. Doyle couldn't shift Booth when he did regain fitness, and with thirty-nine appearances, it was his most profitable campaign in four years.

Booth just slipped in when needed, did his job effectively and if he was dropped, never made a public song and dance about it. That also meant a lot to the fans, because clearly wearing the Manchester City shirt meant more to him than anything else, including personal glory.

The 1977–78 season was his last major contribution to City. He played just 20 times during the turbulent season when Malcolm Allison returned (1978–79) and 24 the season after that. In his final campaign, he played another 30 games, and it was his goal at Peterborough in the FA Cup fifth round that helped City on their way to the 1981 FA Cup final – it was also his last-ever strike for the Blues.

Booth didn't play at Wembley but what a fitting epilogue to his career with the club it would have been if he had done. He would also have set a new record for a City player appearing in Wembley finals but will instead be forever stuck on four with Mike Doyle.

He left for Preston after almost two decades with City, making his final appearance in October 1981 away to Birmingham. Two weeks later, he was a Preston North End player after £30,000 exchanged hands, hailing the end of a Maine Road era.

NO. 35: THE SCALLYWAG SCOUSER –

TONY COLEMAN

SIGNED: 1967 from Doncaster Rovers, £110,000
LEFT: 1969 for Sheffield Wednesday
CROWD IDOL RATING: * *
NICKNAME: 'TC'
APPEARANCES: 102 (+2 sub)
GOALS: 16
SPECIALITY: Finding trouble
FLAWS: Suspect temperament

TC's tale: Punching a referee, throwing furniture out of a window at Lilleshall and generally causing mayhem wherever he went – meet Tony Coleman, the Scouse winger who arrived to play his role in City's halcyon days before moving on like the free spirit he undoubtedly was.

Coleman was regarded, in football circles, as trouble. He had a reputation for mischief making and had served a lengthy ban from the game for giving a ref a right-hook on one occasion! He was also, of course, a very good footballer, and Malcolm Allison was acutely aware of what the player could bring to the City team down the right-hand side. City paid £110,000 for Coleman, who arrived in March 1967 in time to make his debut against Leeds at Elland Road in a goalless draw.

The Kippax loved his cocky swagger and bad-boy reputation – plus he was one of the first players to sport a genuine 'Beatles haircut', though he looked more like a gritty method actor from any number of northern kitchen-sink dramas of the era.

In season 1967–68, Coleman added balance and poise to

City's attacks but was a feisty devil – part of a team of winners, and despite his wayward nature, he'd found his spiritual home. The club he'd joined was just like he was – unpredictable, mesmeric with a propensity to delight and infuriate in equal measure.

As Joe Mercer's side clicked into an unstoppable groove, Coleman was doing his bit, though rarely stealing the limelight from the likes of Bell, Summerbee and Lee. He seldom scored vital winners, but he was playing his part to the full, and as the Blues began their final push for the championship, Coleman missed two games against Chelsea and Wolves and City failed to score in either of them.

As the championship medals were dished out, he'd earned his as much as anybody else. He played much of the less glorious 1968-69 campaign, appearing in 42 of City's league and cup games that year, but he fell out of favour for the 1969–70 campaign, as he had done at many of his previous clubs, and played his final game for City in a League Cup tie against Liverpool, his hometown club, in October 1969. That was the end for TC, who then left Maine Road to seek his fortune at Sheffield Wednesday, but, of course, it didn't last that long and he gradually faded from the scene altogether.

Perhaps fittingly, of all the Glory Years team, it is Coleman who has proved most elusive. He's not been seen around the club for decades, and there were various reports of him living in South Africa, while others have him residing in Australia. There was even a recent rumour that he'd surfaced in Ireland. Wherever he is, he is a true City enigma – perhaps the finest – and it's only right he remains as mysterious today as he ever was in his pomp.

NO. 34: THE GREY ASSASSIN – PETER REID

SIGNED: 1989 from QPR (free)

LEFT: Retired and became manager

CROWD IDOL RATING: * *

NICKNAME: 'Reidy'

APPEARANCES: 100 (+14 as sub)

GOALS: 2

SPECIALITY: Defying the laws of age

GREAT GOAL: Striking home the ball after it'd rebounded off the post against Aston Villa

UNFORGETTABLE MOMENT: Reception following Kendall's resignation

FLAWS: Overly loyal to certain members of his backroom staff?

Reidy's tale: There were numerous reasons the City fans loved Peter Reid. He arrived at the wrong end of a career that had seen him enjoy more than a decade at the top but gave everything for the club that had saved his career from fizzling out quietly at QPR, playing for four magnificent seasons at Maine Road.

When Howard Kendall was appointed as the new manager of the Blues in November 1989, he wanted only one man to be his voice out on the pitch – Peter Reid. He brought him in as player-coach, and Reid revelled in the added duty, finding new life in his ageing legs. The Blues instantly took on a militarised, well-drilled look (as well as an uncanny resemblance to an Everton Vets' team). With Field Marshal Reid in charge, a team that had shipped silly goals and been considered something of a soft touch were unrecognisable.

The thirty-three year old rarely managed the full ninety minutes, but he often embarrassed players ten years younger with his work rate during the time he was on the pitch. City lost just four of their remaining twenty league games and comfortably avoided the threatened drop. It hadn't been pretty to watch, but it had been effective, leaving supporters scratching their heads – was it entertaining unpredictability they really craved or steady, unimaginative results-driven football? It was the former that won hands down – it's in the blood, isn't it?

Kendall quit Maine Road three months into the 1990–91 season, mumbling something about a love affair and a marriage, and while names were suggested as a possible replacement, the City fans wanted only one man . . . and that was enough for chairman Peter Swales. Peter Reid was the club's new manager.

Shortly into his reign as boss, the Blues lost four league games in five, but six wins in the final eight games gave City a fifth-place finish – one place ahead of Manchester United. For that alone, Reid's credit rating soared, and his immediate future was guaranteed.

The 1991–92 season was an odd one, with unbeaten runs followed by several defeats in a row; in short, Reid had become part of the furniture in a very short space of time. He spent the bulk of his transfer budget on defence, with Keith Curle arriving for £2.5 million from Wimbledon, and thanks to four wins on the trot at the end of the campaign, fifth place was achieved again. Reid played 31 times in the league and was now aged 36, but he gave it one last go the season after, although, once again, his side were dogged by loss sequences followed by unbeaten runs.

The winning streak that had seen them end the previous two seasons on a high was absent in 1992–93 and two wins from the last ten gave City a ninth-place finish in the inaugural Premiership campaign. A morale-sapping 5–2 home defeat on the final day to Everton suggested Reid needed to act quickly to halt the slide, and there were calls for a new coach to replace his right-hand man, Sam Ellis. It was strongly felt that Ellis advocated the long-ball game and liked the teams he was involved in to have a strong physical presence. It was he who became the enemy when things began to go pear-shaped, but perhaps it was just that Reid was so well liked, and the fans found it difficult to turn on the man whose appointment they had called for in the first place.

However, Reid would not be swayed, and when the 1993–94 season began badly, the manager and coach were sacked by 'I'm in charge' John Maddocks, many believing that his refusal to replace Ellis was the final straw for the board.

Reid had notched up more than 100 appearances while with City, and his influence on an ailing side made for a pleasant few seasons in the early nineties. He remains one of the best free transfers the club have acquired, and his efforts as player, coach and manager will be fondly remembered.

NO. 33: CAPTAIN FANTASTIC – TONY BOOK

SIGNED: 1966 from Plymouth Argyle, £17,000

LEFT: 1974, retired to backroom staff

CROWD IDOL RATING: * *

NICKNAME: 'Skip'

APPEARANCES: 312 (+3 as sub)

GOALS: 5

SPECIALITY: Snuffing out dangerous wingers

GREAT GOAL: Any goal was great for Tony who averaged one every sixty starts!

UNFORGETTABLE MOMENT: Lifting the championship trophy at St. James' Park in 1968 as City captain

Skip's tale: Tony Book must have thought league football had passed him by when he began yet another season with his hometown club Bath City in the Southern Premier League. Despite interest from a number of clubs during his time at Twerton Park, nothing ever materialised and he was now past his 30th birthday.

Malcolm Allison had been impressed with Book's reliability and leadership during his time as Bath's manager, and when he was invited to take control of Toronto for the summer months, he promised Book he would arrange for him to join him in Canada once he had settled in. A few weeks passed before Book received a call, as promised, from Big Mal, and a few days later, he was playing for Toronto All-Stars.

Book hugely enjoyed his time there, but Allison soon had to fly back to England after being offered the manager's job at Plymouth. Again, he didn't forget about Book and returned to Bath to make him his first signing for Argyle, though he told the

Home Park board the defender was 28, not 30! It had taken an age (pardon the pun) to achieve his ambition of league football, and it was a time when most players were starting to consider retirement, but Tony Book was a special case, and his story is, in many ways, a one-off or, better still, a fairy tale. Playing league football was just reward for his dedication and commitment at non-league level and proof that it is never too late to realise a dream. Allison moved on, becoming Joe Mercer's No. 2 at Maine Road, and two highly successful seasons later, Book was again signed by Big Mal. Despite being 32 years old, he was snapped up for £17,000.

Initially reluctant to sign the ageing defender, Joe Mercer finally conceded that he himself hadn't signed for Arsenal until he'd turned 31, so he was living proof of what could be achieved at what was considered an advanced age for a footballer. Book made his debut away to Southampton in August 1966, just a few weeks after England had lifted the World Cup, and things just got better and better for the quiet former bricklayer from Bath who liked nothing more than a smoke and a bottle of stout in his local. In fact, if his story ended there, it would still be quite a tale. But, of course, there was more to come – much, much more.

After just one full season with City, Book became captain following his good mate Johnny Crossan's move to Middlesbrough. His first campaign as skipper saw City crowned Division One champions with a remarkable 4–3 win at Newcastle on the final day of the season. It was just the beginning of the most glorious period in the club's history.

Book missed the first half of the 1968–69 season with an Achilles injury but then recovered to lift the FA Cup with a 1–0 win over Leicester City, and he was then named Football

Writers' Association (FWA) Player of the Year, an award he shared with Dave Mackay. In his third campaign, he lifted the League Cup and the European Cup-Winners' Cup within the space of six unforgettable weeks – his third and fourth trophies in three years as captain – not bad for a 35 year old in only his fifth season in league football.

That would be the end of the major trophies for Book as a player, but although his bones were getting older, he continued to defy the odds and missed just two games during the 1971–72 season, playing thirty league games the following year before officially retiring during the 1973–74 campaign.

With Mercer and Allison now gone, Johnny Hart had taken over but had been forced to step aside through ill health. Book was the logical choice to step in until a new man was found, and when Ron Saunders became the new manager, he asked Book to be his assistant and hang up his boots. Book agreed but later regretted not playing on a little longer.

Saunders' reign was largely disastrous, and he was sacked before the end of the campaign. This time, thanks to a players' committee, chairman Peter Swales gave Book the job for keeps, and one of his first tasks was to oversee the 1–0 win at Old Trafford that condemned Manchester United to the Second Division. His credit rating with the City fans went through the roof!

But, in truth, while Book was never a Marsh, Summerbee or Lee character, he was still a Crowd Idol in his own way. He had the total respect of the supporters, players and board, and his fellow professionals thought he was a bit special, too. George Best once declared that Book was the most difficult opponent he had to play against – quite an accolade.

He went on to manage the club with great dignity and turned

an ageing side headed in the wrong direction into a genuine force again – no mean achievement – and his judgement in the transfer market was excellent and shrewd. In later years, despite being poorly treated towards the end of his managerial reign when Malcolm Allison was brought back with little or no consultation with Book, he returned to oversee a wonderful crop of youngsters who went on to lift the FA Youth Cup in 1986 and was later a coach under Peter Reid.

It's doubtful there will ever be another Tony Book story at City, or anywhere else for that matter. He is unique in modern-day football – and not bad for £17,000!

NO. 32: IMRE BANANA – IMRE VARADI

SIGNED: 1986 from West Brom, £50,000
LEFT: 1988 for Sheffield Wednesday, £50,000
CROWD IDOL RATING: * *
NICKNAME: 'Imre Banana', 'Olly' (Olly Varadi!)
APPEARANCES: 68 (+13 as sub)
GOALS: 31
SPECIALITY: Finishing
SONG: 'Imre, Imre Banana, Imre Banana, Imre Bana-a-na, hey!'
CATCHPHRASE: 'You've got to pick a pocket or two, my dear'
UNFORGETTABLE MOMENT: That first Kippax banana
FLAWS: Age was against him

Imre's tale: When you think of good, honest, value for money, you have to at least consider the merits of Imre Varadi, who led City's forward line so well for two seasons in the late '80s. He was the archetypal journeyman footballer, yet despite playing for 15 clubs during his 18-year career, he never bettered the statistics he created in his time at Maine Road.

He was picked up for a bargain £50,000 by Jimmy Frizzell following City's disastrous start to the 1986–87 season – the team played ten games and failed to score in half a dozen of them. Varadi signed from West Brom, and when he scored on his debut at Chelsea, it was a taste of things to come. Though City failed to score in twenty of their thirty-six league and cup matches that season, Varadi top scored with nine in twenty-nine league games – or one quarter of all goals scored by the Blues that season (just thirty-six).

Frizzell was sacked and Mel Machin took charge, but the former Norwich boss could see the value of Varadi, and he banked on him and Paul Stewart scoring enough goals to win City's place back in the top division. Varadi and Stewart racked up 16 goals between them in the first 16 games before Varadi picked up an injury, ruling him out of the next match against Huddersfield Town. What happened in that game is now part

Imre Varadi – the City fans went bananas for Imre – literally

of City folklore and Varadi had to watch from the stands as his teammates banged ten goals past Huddersfield.

Varadi won his place back a couple of games later, but seven losses in the next nine games meant there would be no promotion party come May. It was around this time that the odd inflatable banana appeared on the Kippax, and this was put down by many to the fact that people called City's No. 9 'Imre Banana'. It was the start of an inflatable craze that put a much needed smile back on the face of football in England, with City fans inspiring clubs up and down the land to take their own versions of inflatables to their clubs. Stoke had pink panthers, Norwich had canaries and from a whole host of others, perhaps Grimsby Town's 'Harry the Haddock' was the best.

All this was seemingly down to a few Blues fans' interpretation of Varadi's name, and, years later, he admitted it was something he was extremely proud to have been connected with.

City pushed for a late promotion run in 1988 but finished ninth. Trevor Morley was signed the following season and took over Varadi's No. 9 shirt. The writing was on the wall for Imre and, just like the Littlest Hobo, it was time to leave the home comforts he'd craved for so long and find a new family to look after him. Varadi was snapped up by one of his former clubs, Sheffield Wednesday, for the same fee he'd signed for City. Averaging very nearly a goal every other game, Imre was worth every penny City spent on him and a few more, and, bearing in mind the inflatable craze he effectively began, it is no wonder he finishes so high on our Crowd Idol list.

NO. 31: THE PREDATOR – CLIVE ALLEN

SIGNED: 1989 from Bordeaux, £1.1 million

LEFT: 1991 for Chelsea, £250,000

CROWD IDOL RATING: * *

APPEARANCES: 42 (+26 as sub)

GOALS: 21

SPECIALITY: Basically, goal-hanging

GREAT GOAL: His last-minute thunderbolt at Chelsea, in off the underside of the bar

UNFORGETTABLE MOMENT: Climbing off the bench to score twice at Notts County

FLAWS: His shoot-on-sight policy didn't always work – it just did most of the time

Clive's tale: When Mel Machin convinced the City board to part with £1.1 million to bring one of the greatest natural finishers in English football to Maine Road, it was a smart piece of business. Allen had tried a brief foray into French football but, never one to stay somewhere he wasn't entirely happy, wanted a move home, and when City moved in, he was more than happy to don the pale blue shirt.

Allen had made his name at QPR and Crystal Palace before signing for Spurs. He'd actually spent two months as an Arsenal player during the summer but moved on without ever kicking a ball! Must have been the colour of the shirts or something. At White Hart Lane he became a legend, scoring 60 goals in 97 league starts, although he was – incredibly – overlooked by England throughout his career.

He arrived at City with nothing to prove but a lethal reputation to uphold. He failed to score in any of his first four games for the Blues but rolled home the winner in his fifth match – ironically against his old employers QPR. He was then out for the next three games and missed out on the epic 5–1 win over Manchester United that season. He announced his return by scoring two goals from the bench in the next two games. City then managed just four goals in the next six games – Allen scored them all, meaning that he'd now scored seven times in fourteen starts – not bad at all for a striker who was still only twenty-eight.

But when Machin was sacked and Howard Kendall came in, the whole shape of the team altered, and Allen's role steadily diminished. Kendall brought in Adrian Heath and Wayne Clarke (for some reason), and the former Everton pair competed with Allen for the No. 9 shirt. When Allen did start, he was invariably hauled off at some point. In fact, he rarely completed 90 minutes under Kendall, who obviously thought the former Spurs man didn't have enough of a team ethic to play in his side. The free-flowing attacking football under Machin was replaced by the ultra-cautious workmanlike displays under Kendall. It wasn't riveting, but, in fairness, it kept City in the top flight.

Unfortunately, things were about to take a turn for the worse for Allen. During the 1990–91 season, Kendall bought Niall Quinn, and with David White the preferred strike partner to the new man, Allen was substitute for ten of the first fourteen games and completely left out of the remaining four. When Kendall left, Peter Reid continued the trend but at least gave him eight starts after Christmas. The writing was very clearly on the wall, however, and despite the City fans calling Allen's name continuously as the unpopular Heath tried his best, Reid would not buckle and left Allen out of the side until he put him on the bench for the October trip to Notts County. Knowing Reid's famed stubbornness, it probably made him more determined to play Heath in preference.

Running on to a rapturous welcome at Meadow Lane from the travelling Blues, Allen scored twice in a couple of minutes to turn the game around and City won 3–1. The frustrated striker reeled away emotionally, kissing his badge (generally not recommended) to the delight of the Blue army. But he was dropped completely for the next three games. Had Reid taken the celebrations to be a personal dig at him? Only he could say.

With respect to Heath, Allen was the player the fans wanted, and he had the pedigree and record to back up his claims. In fact, in just a few minutes against Notts County, Clive Allen equalled the tally Adrian Heath managed in – get this – 65 games.

Allen deserved better – far better – and while everyone knew he wouldn't get in the mix in a midfield ruck or track back 50 yards and clear the ball from his own box – as Heath might have done – that wasn't Allen's game and neither was it the reason Machin had bought him.

He was there to score goals – end of story. When Chelsea put a paltry offer of £250,000 in, Reid, it's probably fair to say, couldn't wait to offload the striker who was, frankly, becoming an embarrassment to his reign.

So what of Allen's stay with City? His record was a goal every other game, and he was just 30 when Chelsea's offer came in. The price smacked of desperation, further proof of the rift between the player and manager. However, it is worth noting that the bond Allen had made with the City fans was probably as strong as at any of his previous clubs.

To perhaps illustrate that Chelsea was no more than an escape route for all concerned, Allen only stayed at Stamford Bridge for four months before joining West Ham for a year – his record at both clubs being a goal every other game. Incidentally, to prove he'd left Maine Road on the cheap, some four years after leaving City and now aged 32, Allen joined Millwall (his seventh London club) from the Hammers for £750,000.

That was pretty much it for Clive Allen, though he had a brief spell at Carlisle before calling it a day and becoming an occasional TV pundit.

30–21

FIRST-TEAM REGULARS

NO. 30: THE ARTFUL DODGER – PETER BEAGRIE

SIGNED: 1994 from Everton, £1.1 million
LEFT: 1997 for Bradford City, £200,000
CROWD IDOL RATING: * * *
NICKNAME: 'Beags'
APPEARANCES: 58 (+7 as sub)
GOALS: 5
SPECIALITY: Torturing full-backs
UNFORGETTABLE MOMENT: Any of his back-flip goal celebrations
FLAWS: Not many, although he liked to beat a defender so many times
he sometimes forgot the whole point was to cross for a striker to score

Beags' story: Part of the Horton trio signed just before the deadline to keep City up in 1993–94, Peter Beagrie became an almost instant Crowd Idol when he first played for City. Beagrie was a defender's worst nightmare, able to wriggle away from any full-back with ease and then fire over superb crosses. He was something close to a genius, and it's a sad indictment of English football that he never came close to winning an England cap in all his time in the top division.

Any team containing Beagrie needed to be feared because, on his day, he could destroy sides single-handed – and often did. He made his debut in a 0–0 draw at Oldham's Boundary Park and then played his part in a 2–2 draw with Ipswich Town. For his home debut, he captivated a sparse Maine Road by scoring one and providing an endless stream of perfect crosses for the other two new signings, Paul Walsh and Uwe Rösler. In fact, Horton's decision to sign the three forwards was nothing short of inspired, and all three played their part in City's survival that season.

But if there had been plenty of pressure in those closing weeks of the campaign, the 1994–95 season was all about attacking, free-spirited football – and the Blues' supporters lapped it up. Ironically, the Kippax was closed, having been demolished, and the majority of fans were rehoused in the North Stand. For around five months, the football on view would have had even the most hard-to-please City fan drooling. It was eye-candy of the highest order and conducting the orchestra was inevitably Beagrie and his limitless array of party tricks.

Maine Road, so often the venue of easy pickings for visiting sides over the previous few years, became a fortress, a place to fear for opposition defences. With the North Stand more than making up for the loss of the Kippax, there was a noisy, partisan atmosphere at home games that hadn't been prevalent for many years. Beagrie, in particular, seemed to revel in it, saving the best of his showboating for the North Stand end. The first ten games yielded six wins and four draws with twenty-six goals for City and eleven conceded – thirty-seven goals at an average of almost four per match.

It was an amazing time and a period that everybody knew had its sell-by date. Had the Blues kept it up, they would have won the Premiership – that's why fans knew something would give! The season gradually petered away, and failure to score in a half-dozen home games after Christmas ultimately cost Horton his job.

With Horton gone, City employed Alan Ball, and thanks mainly to a lengthy injury absence, Beagrie only played a handful of games more before joining Bradford City for just £200,000 in 1997 – a fee that angered many of the fans who felt he was worth much more. Plus, everyone knew that he'd been out for so long it would take time to get him somewhere near his best again.

Ball didn't have the patience, and, in truth, Beagrie was probably happy to have a fresh start with the Bantams. He enjoyed a terrific four-year spell at Valley Parade before finding his way to Scunthorpe United, where he was a player-coach up to the 2005–06 season, returning to say 'thanks' in the colours of The Iron in an FA Cup third-round tie in 2006. An entertainer and excellent footballer: they don't make 'em like Beags anymore!

NO. 29: THE GLASWEGIAN GROWLER – GERRY GOW

SIGNED: 1980 from Bristol City, £200,000

LEFT: 1982 for Rotherham, £100,000

CROWD IDOL RATING: * * *

APPEARANCES: 36

GOALS: 7

SPECIALITY: Bone-crunching tackles

SONG: 'Gerry Gow, Gerry Gow, Gerry Gow . . .'

CATCHPHRASE: 'Can yer ma stitch?'

GREAT GOAL: 25-yard free-kick v. Norwich City, January 1981

UNFORGETTABLE MOMENT: The 'you want some, pal?' stare he gave
a Tottenham fan who had run on the pitch to confront him in the 1981
FA Cup final

FLAWS: Missed too many games through injury

Gerry's story: Gerry Gow – a name to turn quivering forwards
to jelly at the thought of a possible 50-50 challenge. And rightly
so – Gow arrived at Maine Road in October 1980 as part of
John Bond's mini-Tartan Army with the intention of giving an
ailing City team some much-needed backbone.

He'd been around quite a while but was well respected within
the game. Gow, along with Bobby McDonald and Tommy
Hutchison, would become the catalysts in an amazing turnaround
in the Blues' fortunes, the team climbing from the foot of the
table to tenth position and winning a place in the 1981 Centenary
FA Cup final against Spurs. Gow was inspirational in midfield,
winning tackles he had no right to win and lifting his teammates
and the crowd when games were finely balanced. In the autumn
of his career, he'd found a club and supporters who appreciated
everything he did or attempted to do, and he must have perhaps

rued the fact he was at the wrong end of his playing days.

The Glasgow-born No. 8 loved nothing better than a good scrap but had many more strings to his bow than just being a ball winner. He could pass well and was a real threat from any set piece around the opposition's box. In short, he was a quality player with an edge to his game.

He became popular from day one, taking over the shirt of the ineffective Steve Daley and adding a new dimension to the team, growling out instructions to the younger players and leading by example. The City fans quickly related to his blood-and-thunder attitude and regularly

Gerry Gow – all perm and gnashing teeth

chanted his name after he'd left some poor sap prostrate due to an explosive, but almost always fair, tackle. He looked like somebody you wouldn't want to meet on a darkened street in Paisley with his grey straggly perm and moustache but he was the type of character you would want alongside you in the trenches. Injury meant he played only a handful of games the following season, and after battling his way back to fitness, he was sold to Rotherham United. He felt aggrieved at not being given the chance to continue his City career, but though his star shone briefly at Maine Road, it burned with an intense glow and warmed all those who were lucky enough to witness it.

NO. 28: THE BLOND BOMBSHELL – COLIN HENDRY

SIGNED: 1989 from Blackburn, £700,000

LEFT: 1991 for Blackburn, £700,000

CROWD IDOL RATING: * * *

APPEARANCES: 70 (+7 as sub)

GOALS: 10

GREAT GOAL: His one-two and neat finish against United in 1990

UNFORGETTABLE MOMENT: The celebration for the goal listed above

Colin's tale: Very few central defenders attained quite the popularity that Colin Hendry managed during his all-too-brief stay with Manchester City. The Scottish powerhouse arrived shortly after Mel Machin was sacked following a 6–0 defeat to Derby County and presumably Machin had brokered the deal. It was, therefore, an odd set of circumstances that Hendry found himself in on his arrival at Maine Road. It was another month before Howard Kendall took the vacant post with the Blues, but with Hendry as a lynchpin, the defence soon became one of the meanest in the division.

Hendry won the fans over with his fearless attitude and willingness to go in where it hurt. With his shock of white blond hair, Hendry cut a dashing figure for the Blues. He also loved to join the attack and managed several goals in his first 25 league games for City. The following season he only scored one – but what a goal it was. In fact, it looked like the goal that would probably seal the Manchester derby as he played a one-two and then coolly slid the ball home to put City 3–1 up, leaving Hendry to wheel away in delight – an act some Reds wrongly connected with the Munich air disaster. United rallied and the game ended 3–3, and within a couple of weeks, Kendall quit City to take over as boss of Everton.

Peter Reid was installed as manager, and, for a while, Hendry continued at the heart of the Blues' defence, forging a useful partnership with Steve Redmond. But Reid, it seemed, wanted his own men in defence and began to build a side in his own image. During the close season he purchased centre-back Keith Curle and full-back Terry Phelan from Wimbledon for around £5 million and it was Hendry, not Redmond, who made way for Curle. Hendry was out of the picture and would only play six games from the bench before returning to Blackburn for the same fee City had originally paid – £700,000 – a price most City fans felt was a give-away.

In fact, the fans voiced their support of Hendry whether he was on the pitch or not, in what must have been an uncomfortable time for both Curle and Peter Reid, but he was never in the starting line-up again, and his last appearance was away to Southampton in a 3–0 win at The Dell.

It's unclear whether Reid had a personality clash with Hendry or not, but a similar fate befell another hero of the time, Clive Allen. Snubbing both these players didn't exactly boost Reid's popularity, but he was already in credit with the City fans, and he just about rode the storm.

Hendry went on to enjoy a terrific second spell with Blackburn and was generally afforded a warm reception on his return. But question marks over Reid's judgement remained, especially when the following season he signed unknown Dutch centre-back Michel Vonk and sold off the popular Redmond. City's fortunes hardly improved, and the club instead went into steady decline. In short, selling Hendry was a big mistake.

NO. 27: MIDFIELD SCHEMER – GARY OWEN

SIGNED: 1974 from Manchester Boys

LEFT: 1979 for West Brom, £450,000

CROWD IDOL RATING: * * *

APPEARANCES: 122 (+2 as sub)

GOALS: 23

SPECIALITY: Free-kicks and penalties

UNFORGETTABLE MOMENT: His emotional return to Maine Road in September 1979 when he orchestrated a 4–0 win for the Baggies

Owen's story: Born in the rugby stronghold that is St Helens, Gary Owen is an honorary Mancunian. His ties to City, like so many former players who left to play elsewhere, remain strong to this day.

Snapped up while playing for Manchester Boys, Owen had to earn his corn in the youth and reserve teams before finally winning his first-team spurs aged only 17 against Wolves at Maine Road in 1976. The Blues won 3–2, and he added three more starts before the summer.

Manager Tony Book saw the tidy midfielder as a natural successor to Alan Oakes, who had finally severed his ties with City by signing for Chester. Owen, with his cultured left foot, took on the No. 6 shirt and won instant praise for his mature performances throughout his first full season. Book's faith paid dividends as the youngster played 31 league matches, whilst the Blues finished runners-up to Liverpool. With Peter Barnes, Asa Hartford and Paul Power, Book couldn't have wished for a more talented or industrious midfield quartet, and they were the beating heart of a very formidable mid-'70s team.

The following season, Owen upped his goal tally by taking

over as penalty-taker and he ended the campaign with seven in thirty-three league games as City again qualified for Europe by finishing fourth. Along with Barnes, Owen was the golden boy of the side and could do no wrong in the eyes of the fans.

City and England coach Bill Taylor compared Owen's skills to that of Brazilian legend Dirceu, and he seemed to be a future captain of the club, winning ten caps for the England Under-21s, too. Despite the Blues' poor 1978–79 campaign, Owen finished joint-top scorer with then record buy Mike Channon, having notched 15 goals.

Some felt that a senior England call-up and the City captaincy beckoned for Owen, who probably couldn't have been happier with his lot. However, Malcolm Allison's return as first-team coach was to spell the end for Owen and fellow Crowd Idol Barnes. Just two days after the end of the season, Barnes was sold to West Brom, and, in an incredibly ill-judged move by Allison, Owen, aged twenty-one, was sold to the same club just thirteen days later.

To say Owen was reluctant to leave was an understatement and the frustration and anger he felt at a critical point in his development arguably cost him a senior call-up for England. He cried the day Ron Atkinson arrived to take him to The Hawthorns, unable to understand why he was being sold. What had he done wrong, he wondered? The answer, of course, was nothing. Perhaps his only crime was that he was an established star, and Allison appeared to be hell-bent on creating a new team from untried youngsters and lower-league players nobody had ever heard of.

Dave Watson, Asa Hartford and Mike Channon would all follow Owen and Barnes out of Maine Road during a period that still beggars belief. Owen managed to get back on track with the Baggies, though he was always reserved a special reception on his returns to Maine Road by the supporters who knew he'd never wanted to leave.

He won 22 Under-21 caps in all – one of the most decorated players ever at that level – and things went well enough with Albion, but during the 1984–85 season he broke his ankle twice and contracted meningitis. He returned to the first team a year later but found it hard to become a regular so left for Panionios in Greece, staying for a year before playing a handful of games for Sheffield Wednesday. He called it quits in Cyprus in 1989 following a brief spell with APOEL Nicosia, at the relatively young age of 31.

He later became an art dealer and is the resident City legend on Century FM's evening football show, a position he's held for several years. Some callers to the show, mainly United fans, have questioned Owen's right to be labelled a City 'legend', and based on his time and appearances with the Blues, they have a point. However, few would deny that, but for his enforced transfer away from Maine Road, he almost certainly would have earned that tag and at least deserves the title 'honorary legend'.

NO. 26: THE MAGICIAN – EYAL BERKOVIC

SIGNED: 2001 from Celtic, £1.5 million

LEFT: 2003 for Portsmouth, free

CROWD IDOL RATING: * * *

NICKNAME: 'Berko'

APPEARANCES: 56 (+11 as sub)

GOALS: 9

MOMENT IN TIME: Solo run and goal v. Norwich when City were down to ten men

SPECIALITY: Vision, eye-of-the-needle passing and spectacular goal celebrations

SONG: 'Eyal, Eyal Berko-vic, Eyal Berko-vic!'

NOT A LOT OF PEOPLE KNOW THAT: Eyal used to own a caf in Prestwich Village

FLAWS: Suspect temperament and scared of getting hurt

Eyal's story: There have been a number of players who have played for both City and West Ham – two footballing academies whose supporters like their football to be easy on the eye – during their careers, and Eyal Berkovic is such a case. A supremely gifted midfielder, Berkovic arrived from Israel to carve out a reputation at Southampton before being snapped up by Harry Redknapp for the Hammers.

Following a training ground fracas with John Hartson, he headed north of the border and joined Celtic, where his fiery personality soon rubbed the Parkhead fans up the wrong way – he allegedly made one comment that Celtic should be more like Rangers in their mentality and outlook, which was not a wise move.

From that point on, things went downhill, and whether an

Eyal Berkovic – explosive talent and temperament to match –
matched incredible vision with intelligence on the pitch

apology would have smoothed things over is doubtful; besides, Eyal didn't do apologies and had a tendency to feel the forces of fate were conspiring against him. He went on loan to Blackburn Rovers and at a time City were crying out for a creative midfielder, Joe Royle decided not to move for the player.

Rumours were that Celtic boss Martin O'Neill had hinted that Berkovic was a disruptive influence and that was enough for Joe – though surely O'Neill would have been more likely to want rid of such a disruptive influence rather than put off prospective suitors. Royle was sacked, and Kevin Keegan made Berkovic one of his first signings for just £1.5 million, a third of the price Celtic had paid West Ham – a genuine bargain fee for a special talent. Keegan didn't care that additional baggage came with the Israeli – he just saw that he was a very good player available for a knock-down price.

Keegan's first game in charge saw Stuart Pearce at the back and Berkovic in midfield for the visit of Watford. It was an electrically charged evening at Maine Road, and the Blues fairly crackled on the night, the team inspired by the little Israeli who immediately looked at home.

His clever finish capped a mesmerising debut, and he lapped up the fans' acclaim, running over to the Kippax to celebrate his goal. He was injured shortly after, and in his absence, Keegan brought in Algerian star Ali Benarbia on a free transfer. Though two similarly styled playmakers, Keegan stated in an interview that he intended to play both Berkovic and Benarbia in the team, memorably saying, 'People ask how could I pick both players to play in the same side – I ask, why not?'

It was a bold but intelligent move by Keegan, and he was rewarded when the Muslim and the Israeli – only City could have such a potentially explosive combination and get away with it – commenced taking apart the hapless defences of the First Division. Their talents would have befitted any Premiership, Serie A or La Liga side. Ali and Eyal were just too hot to handle, but there were some people who felt that Berkovic played even better when he was the sole creative force.

At perhaps his most breathtaking best, Berkovic ran alone towards the Norwich City box tracked by three defenders with City down to ten men. He dummied, dropped a shoulder and then poked the ball home in a magnificent solo effort that sent Maine Road wild with delight.

On City's return to the top flight, he ran the game against Manchester United at Old Trafford and was inspirational in the last ever Maine Road derby, when City beat the Reds 3–1 – the sight of Eyal telling the United contingent to 'ssshhh!' will long be remembered.

Yet things turned sour very quickly. When Berkovic (not unreasonably) asked for a new deal with one year left on his current contract, the player and manager somehow fell out, and the word was that when you fell out with Keegan, there was no way back. A pantomime was played before the press with Keegan claiming he had no axe to grind with the player, but the Israeli's days were clearly numbered. Many City fans wondered why, when Ali Benarbia had only recently left, Berkovic was left to rot in the reserves, particularly with the side struggling for invention and creativity in midfield. The signing of Antoine Sibierski was the final straw for Eyal and he played a handful of games before issuing a 'come and get me' message to Harry Redknapp at Portsmouth – something the Pompey manager was only too happy to do – and Eyal left for the south coast on a free transfer. Keegan was desperate to see the back of a player who was becoming an embarrassing exclusion to his side.

Midfielders of Berkovic's ability are few and far between, and the bitter end to his time with the Blues was a real pity: the fans were the only losers. He was petulant, of course – it was in his nature – and who could forget him running a finger across his throat to a woman in the Platt Lane end against Crewe, later claiming she had aimed anti-Semitic abuse at him? His was a flawed genius but nobody could deny his talent. He made his Portsmouth debut against – who else – City, with Keegan adding insult to injury by not stipulating that the player could not immediately face his former club. If ever anyone was going to give their all to gain revenge, it was Berkovic against Keegan. The City fans knew what would happen, and, sure enough, Pompey won 4–2 with Eyal's influence embarrassingly obvious.

When Redknapp quit Fratton Park, Eyal left soon after under the same black cloud that had followed him around during most of his stay in British football. He is now playing out his days in his homeland for Maccabi Haifa.

NO. 25: THE PATRON SAINT OF LOST CAUSES –

PAUL WALSH

SIGNED: 1994 from Portsmouth, £750,000
LEFT: 1995 for Portsmouth, £500,000
CROWD IDOL RATING: * * *
NICKNAME: 'Walshy'
APPEARANCES: 62
GOALS: 19
SPECIALITY: Refusing to give up anything
GREAT GOAL: Terrific finish against former club Spurs in the unforgettable 1993–94 Maine Road goal-fest
UNFORGETTABLE MOMENT: Being allowed to leave the club for no obvious reason

Walshy's tale: When Paul Walsh signed for City for £750,000 from Portsmouth, he helped transform a lightweight attack into a menacing strike force and in doing so, soon had the wholehearted backing of the City fans.

It's probably fair to say that most people didn't realise what Paul Walsh was all about when he first arrived at Maine Road. He'd always been regarded as a useful forward while at Luton, Liverpool and Tottenham, but he wasn't as high profile as some of the strikers around and generally just got on with his job.

In fact, most people didn't know what to expect. Peter Beagrie and Uwe Rösler had also just joined, and with Nick Summerbee on the right and Beagrie on the left, Walsh walked straight into a team that played very much to his strengths. Walsh was skilful on the ground, had a tireless work rate and was excellent in the air. He was, in many ways, the perfect striker.

Paul Walsh – didn't know how to give anything
less than everything for the Blues

He feasted on the superb crossing of the wingers, linked up
well with Rösler and Niall Quinn and began to score regularly.
But City fans love to see their forwards get stuck in and give
their all, and in Walsh they had a player who was prepared
to give everything each time he pulled on the blue jersey. He
seemed to relish every moment of his time with the Blues and
was very much a City player, mixing easy-on-the-eye style with
good, honest sweat.

When he signed in March 1994, Brian Horton had decided
to go for broke with Walsh, Rösler and Beagrie literally scoring
their way out of trouble. Had those three players not been
signed, City would probably have gone down two years earlier
than they actually did. From the moment all three played
together, City lost just once in the final nine games, and to

further illustrate the point, the new boys bagged all but two of the dozen goals scored during the run-in.

The following season, Walsh, Beagrie and Rösler scored 25 of the 42 goals scored in the first half of the campaign with Walsh bagging a dozen of them. By the end of the season, Rösler top scored with twenty-two and Walsh ended with fifteen – a more than fruitful partnership when you consider Niall Quinn weighed in with a respectable ten goals as well. Walsh had missed just four games all season, and Horton seemed to be moulding an exciting all-out attack-minded side that was thrilling the Maine Road crowds – unfortunately reduced in capacity for the most part by more than 30,000 while the Kippax was rebuilt.

But the innovative Horton was sacked and replaced by Alan Ball, and the former England World Cup winner had his own ideas on who should lead his line. Just three games into the new season, he decided to do one of the worst swap deals in history, exchanging the livewire Walsh with Gerry Creaney from Portsmouth in a deal where City actually had to pay another £1 million for the overweight, lumbering striker!

The deal – with both players changing clubs over a three-day period – dumbfounded City fans, who had just seen Georgi Kinkladze arrive, and just about summed up what was ahead for the supporters under the Ball tenure. Creaney made just eight starts in three seasons, scoring five times. Walsh had managed 19 goals in 62 starts in just under a season and a half.

He left Maine Road with his head held high but probably a heavy heart – he should have been at the club for at least another couple of years and would have almost certainly forged an exciting link with Kinky. Alas, we'll never know thanks to Ball's idea of a good deal.

Walsh played on for another two years with Pompey before

retiring from the game aged 35. Today he is part of Sky Sports' *Soccer Saturday* team and still attends City supporter meetings when he gets the chance. As for Creaney? His best years were all spent earlier at Celtic, and he was loaned out four times before being given away to St Mirren. After he left the Blues, he never cost any of the clubs he played for a penny.

NO. 24 TRICKY DICKY – PAUL DICKOV

SIGNED: 1996 from Arsenal, £1 million

LEFT: 2002 to Leicester City, £50,000

CROWD IDOL RATING: * * *

NICKNAME: 'The Wasp', 'Dicky'

APPEARANCES: 122 (+49 as sub)

GOALS: 59

MOMENT IN TIME: The equaliser against Gillingham in 1999 that changed the club's destiny

SPECIALITY: Fifty-fifty tackles with defenders at least two-feet taller than him and gritting his teeth for ninety minutes

NOT A LOT OF PEOPLE KNOW THAT: Dicky spent time on loan at Brighton whilst with Arsenal

Dicky's Story: When Paul Dickov played for City, he was a hero because of his attitude. When he left, he became a pain in the arse because of his attitude. He's a 100 per center who arrived at Maine Road three games into the 1996–97 season for a fee of £1 million. The former Arsenal striker tumbled into the eye of the storm when he made his debut away to Stoke, and he would have the dubious honour of being Alan Ball's last signing as City manager – the Blues lost 2–1 at the Victoria Ground and Ball was sacked a couple of days later. Ball would be the first of five managers Dickov would play under in his first, chaotic season with the Blues, a season during which few, if any, players came out with any real credit.

If the diminutive Glaswegian had left at the end of the campaign, few would have been particularly bothered as City had finished way out of contention for a quick return to the Premiership. Though Dickov got stuck in with the best of them, he wasn't what you'd call a natural finisher, and, at times, it was hard to see where he fitted in, though that could have been said of half-a-dozen players during that period. Joe

Paul Dickov – what he lacked in natural ability he made up for ten-fold with effort and spirit

Royle had become the new manager following Frank Clarke's spectacularly unspectacular time as boss, but he couldn't prevent the club sinking to the Second Division (the nation's third tier) for the first time in their history.

Dickov's story really began in season 1998–99. With City

losing to Stoke at Maine Road, he was one of two substitutes brought on by Royle to spice things up with the team still floundering in midtable like a ship without a rudder. Dickov and Tony Vaughan – the other sub against Stoke – got stuck in, brought the crowd to life and the Blues won the game 2–1. He was the jump lead on a flat battery and once revved up, City finally got their act together and scraped into the play-offs.

Dickov got the goal that erased Wigan's lead in the first leg of the semi-final and, of course, also scored in the play-off final against Gillingham. When the ball fell to him in the 95th minute of a game City had no right to recover from, he swung his right foot with all his might and scored the goal of his life. From that moment on, Paul Dickov, Saint, became a fact. He even had the temerity to test his loyal subjects shortly after by missing his spot-kick in the shoot-out, but his face said everything. Crestfallen, he showed that he loved the club. That his will to win and enthusiasm for the shirt hadn't resulted in a successful penalty seemed to totally baffle him. Fortunately, it didn't matter, and City won the day against the gallant Gills.

Dickov seemed to grow another foot in height as they powered their way back to the Premiership, and he scored the fourth goal of the win at Blackburn that finally clinched the second promotion spot on the last day of the season. Arguably, that was the last real high Dicky enjoyed at City. Of course, there were moments when the crowd chanted his name while the likes of George Weah or Paulo Wanchope were poncing about up front in the ensuing years, but his days were numbered the minute Kevin Keegan became manager. The Paul Dickovs of this world were not for Keegan, and he was shipped out to Leicester for a paltry 50 grand.

He returned to a hero's reception when he turned out for

Leicester City at the City of Manchester Stadium, but then ruined it by scoring and celebrating as he always had done in the past – with passion and aggression. That upset a few people, but his goal against Gillingham was later voted the 'best ever' by supporters, and he officially entered the club's Hall of Fame. While he was a Blue, he gave his all every time he played. He'll never enjoy playing his football more than he did while he was at City, and few players will give more than he did. For a time, Dicky was perhaps a notch above being a Crowd Idol.

NO. 23: THE HUYTON HUSTLER – JOEY BARTON

SIGNED: Academy junior after release by Everton
LEFT: Still with club as at April 2006
CROWD IDOL RATING: * * *
NICKNAME: 'Joey B'
APPEARANCES: 104 (+11 as sub)
GOALS: 10
SPECIALITY: Non-stop 100 per cent effort, feisty tackling
GREAT GOAL: Spectacular volley v. Wigan, Boxing Day 2005 or 25-yarder v. Charlton, 2006
UNFORGETTABLE MOMENT: Telling the United end to 'shhh!' in the 2005 Old Trafford derby
FLAWS: Temperament has been suspect in the past, but he's worked hard to improve

Joey's tale: The name Joey Barton came to the fore at City for all the wrong reasons, initially. Rejected by his boyhood club Everton and then picked up by City (because the same recruitment officer had moved from Goodison Park to Maine Road and thought he had a chance), things weren't going right for the young Huyton midfielder.

City were all set to release him, too, when somehow he dug a bit deeper and won himself a bit more time. He worked hard, listened to the academy coaches and progressed through to the reserves, where, again, he knuckled down and tried to better himself, all under the watchful eye of manager Kevin Keegan.

Then, with a couple of first-teamers out injured, he was named in the squad that travelled to Middlesbrough in 2002. On the bench, Keegan told him to warm up, then soon after, to get ready to come on. Barton had left his shirt in the dug-out so went

Joey Barton — total commitment on the pitch
with his star continuing to rise at speed

back to retrieve it, but to no avail. He searched everywhere, and then it dawned on him – he'd left the shirt on the bench while everyone was having the half-time chat in the dressing rooms, and an opportunist Boro fan had stolen it. That was that – he couldn't come on because there was no spare shirt for the subs!

Crestfallen, the youngster was ribbed by the senior players all the way back to Manchester, but only because they knew his chance would come again. Until he actually did make his first start for the club against Bolton, Barton's ambition burned away undiminished, and part of him must have wondered if his moment in the sun had passed him mockingly by.

How much that incident made him the player he is today, we will never know. But it could be that to get so close to the first team after almost being released not that long before channelled his mind to not only winning another chance but never letting it go once he did – and that's more or less what happened.

Enthusiastic and full of running, his aggression sometimes spilled over to the point of becoming a liability, and he was not initially an automatic choice for Keegan, who seemed wary of players of his ilk, players such as Paul Dickov and Danny Tiatto who had fire in their belly and constantly found their way into referees' notebooks. Yet Barton was not going to fade back into the reserves, and despite his sometimes wayward distribution and overexuberance, he more and more became a fixture in Keegan's team.

But there were many rocky moments ahead for the young Scouser. His temperament was called into question on numerous occasions, and in a pre-season friendly with Doncaster, he became embroiled in a scuffle with opposition players that led to a very public dressing-down from Keegan. Worse followed. A red card at Tottenham in the FA Cup, with City 3–0 down, infuriated his manager, who'd seen his young charge continue to bicker with referee Rob Styles after the whistle for the break had gone and had warned the young player what the consequences would be. City won that game 4–3 and perhaps changed the course of Barton's destiny forever, with the magnitude of the performance all but dissolving away the memory of his red card.

He was becoming more and more important to the team, yet his off-field antics were still making more headlines than when he actually played. There was an incident with reserve player Jamie Tandy at a Christmas party, and as far as Keegan was concerned, it was last-chance saloon time.

On the pitch, Barton counted his blessings and worked harder than ever. His passing improved, his delivery improved and the number of silly cautions he was picking up decreased. At last the likeable youngster seemed to have turned the corner, and the City fans loved him for it. They knew that every time he went out he would give everything for the shirt, and what more could you ask from a player?

He was also imposing himself much more in games; he'd filled out and seemed much more mature in every aspect of his life. Then, under new boss Stuart Pearce, he became involved in a fracas during a club tour of Thailand. He clashed with a young Everton fan and then allegedly bit the finger of Richard Dunne, who was acting as peacemaker.

He was sent home in disgrace, and this time it appeared his luck had run out. Pearce met with chairman John Wardle to discuss Barton's future, and how close they came to terminating his contract only they know. Pearce, however, insisted that if the player were to come back into the fold, he would have to undergo an anger-management course in order to get himself back on track.

This he did and his performances continued to improve – yet there was still one more devastating blow awaiting Joey when his brother was involved in a racially motivated murder in his hometown of Huyton. Joey made a televised plea for his brother to give himself up, which he duly did.

On the pitch, Joey's influence on the team continued to grow to the point where it was impossible to think of him not playing. Determination, drive, ability and desire, Joey Barton has the lot. He's also had to overcome a number of sizeable hurdles during his career: some of his own making, some not. The end result? A footballer on his way to international recognition, safe in the knowledge that the only way is up, with proof that guts and drive can win the day. His transfer request following a contract negotiation breakdown in January 2006 damaged his reputation with the fans with a large number of supporters feeling he'd let the club down after they'd stood by him through thick and thin. At the time of writing, a new deal looked likely with Joey admitting he'd been a 'bit hasty' and all parties seemed hopeful of a new long-term contract being agreed. Time will tell.

NO. 22: THE TASMANIAN DEVIL – DANNY TIATTO

SIGNED: 1998 from Stoke City, £300,000

LEFT: 2004 for Leicester City, £150,000

CROWD IDOL RATING: * * *

APPEARANCES: 128 (+31 as sub)

GOALS: 4

SPECIALITY: Bone-crunching tackles

SONG: 'Tia-Tia-Tiatto, Tiatto, Tiatto!'

CATCHPHRASE: 'Bagsy first in the bath'

GREAT GOAL: Cracking volley in League Cup away to Derby

UNFORGETTABLE MOMENT: Wonder goal at Middlesbrough, wrongly ruled out for offside

FLAWS: Hair-trigger temper

Danny's tale: City fans loved Danny Tiatto for the same reason managers tore their hair out at him – the fire in his belly was too much for him to contain, and on occasions, he simply 'lost it'.

The Aussie firebrand was at Stoke City (though had been on loan in Switzerland for a time) before Joe Royle paid £300,000 for his services. It took a while for Tiatto to settle in and he was sent off several times in his early days with City, playing little part in the Blues' journey to the play-off final against Gillingham.

Royle deployed Tiatto either in midfield or at full-back, two positions at which the Australian player was equally adept. The manager could clearly see that Tiatto was improving, both in his performances and attitude, and played him more often as City powered their way back to the Premiership in 1999–2000. During 2000–01, he became a regular, filling any role that needed filling and giving 110 per cent each time he played – something the fans certainly picked up on as they voted him their Player of the Year that season.

He still had moments when the red mist took over. You were never quite sure what would spark him into some outrageous tackle, but the supporters loved his wholehearted 'up and at 'em' attitude and forgave his occasional indiscretions. He was no mug either and could play a bit, dribbling on occasions with his head down and going on momentum-powered runs forward. Goals were missing from his game, however, and by the time he left the club, he averaged around one goal every forty games, which isn't good enough for a player of his calibre.

He would always seem to make progress then shoot himself in the foot. He once clattered City teammate Chris Killen in a match between Australia and New Zealand and when Kevin Keegan took over at Maine Road, the new manager pinned Tiatto by the throat after the player was sent off against Norwich and began arguing with the opposing bench as he left the field. There was just no give in him, and in a split-second, he could spoil a great display with an X-rated clash.

Keegan was often furious with Tiatto but played him frequently as City won the First Division with a record haul of points in 2002. But when Blackburn visited Maine Road and Tiatto came on as sub, he flung himself into a nasty challenge on David Thompson and was instantly red carded. Keegan couldn't believe what he'd seen and forced Tiatto to apologise, while suggesting his time with City might be over. The fact the Blues rallied late on from 2–0 down to draw 2–2 eased what could have been game, set and match for the Socceroo. It wasn't quite, but Keegan clearly never trusted Tiatto again and never again gave him a regular starting place, apart from when he was slotted in to replace an injured party. Ironically, his last appearance for City was against the same opponents that had been there at the beginning of the end – Blackburn Rovers – when he came on as substitute in January 2004 for his last game in City colours.

He joined Leicester City later that year but is still fondly remembered by City fans for his feisty days with the Blues. All heart, high energy and high tackles, with not a great deal in between, that was Danny Tiatto – a genuine 110 per center.

NO. 21: THE MAN MOUNTAIN – DAVE WATSON

SIGNED: 1975 from Sunderland, £275,000

LEFT: 1979 for Werder Bremen

CROWD IDOL RATING: * * *

NICKNAME: 'Big Dave'

APPEARANCES: 188

GOALS: 6

SPECIALITY: Aerial ability

UNFORGETTABLE MOMENT: His own goal v. Liverpool 1976

Dave's tale: When Tony Book decided he needed a defensive lynchpin to build his team around, he went for the best available – Dave Watson. Watson was at Sunderland, but the Roker Park side couldn't turn down an offer of £275,000 for their towering centre-back, and in the summer of 1975, Watson signed for the Blues.

He took on the shirt number he was born for – No. 5 – and made his debut in the Anglo-Scottish Cup away to 'McBlackpool' (well who else would you expect to play in the Anglo-Scottish Cup?). By the start of the 1975–76 season, he'd already forged an understanding with central-defensive partner Mike Doyle.

The Watson-Doyle partnership was a fearsome sight for any attacker, and Doyle knew how to get his teammate wound up for battle, occasionally telling him an opposing forward had called him a sissy – whether he had or not. It usually did the trick and added extra vigour to the next few challenges on the hapless target.

City had a much tighter look to them during Watson's first year with the Blues and were also progressing well in the League Cup. By the time City reached the semis, they looked unstoppable, but prior to the first leg away to Middlesbrough, Mike Doyle discovered Watson lying on the floor of the hotel bedroom paralysed in pain.

Dave Watson — somewhere between a rock and a hard face

His back had seized up. He was in absolute agony and was ruled out for several games. But the strapping defender was back for the final and was at his dogged best with Doyle, the pair unsung heroes as City lifted the trophy for the second time in six years. Pictures of Watson playing on with blood spattered on his shirt from a head wound pretty much summed up his attitude to the game. Blood didn't bother a man like Dave

Watson – it was an expendable commodity; in fact, it was almost mandatory that a bit of claret be shed in the line of duty.

Injury sidelined him from the final ten games of the campaign. Up to that point, City had not let in more than two goals in a game. In those matches without Watson, City conceded seventeen goals, including three on two occasions, losing six of them, which ultimately cost the Blues a top-five finish.

However, season 1976–77 would prove a different kettle of fish. The Blues, with Watson and Doyle imperious, kept 12 clean sheets in the first 19 games to establish themselves as one of the favourites for the title. Liverpool were inevitably the main threat and when they visited for the last game of 1976, City led 1–0 with just a few minutes to go. Then, on an icy pitch, a cross came in and Watson knocked the ball past Joe Corrigan into his own net for a dramatic equaliser. Just *how* dramatic would become clearer when the season finished.

City continued pressing for the remainder of the campaign, but when the Blues wrapped up their season with a 1–0 win at Coventry, Liverpool were already confirmed champions – by one point – and Dave Watson would be unavoidably forever linked with the 'what if?' theories because of his own goal. Of course, he didn't cost City the title – it was his consistency that helped the Blues become such a tough nut to crack in the first place, and the title was lost elsewhere that season – two 3–1 defeats to Manchester United and a crushing 4–0 defeat at Derby, for instance, were far more damaging to the cause.

Watson's presence was immense as City had another crack at the title in 1977–78, but he had to get along without Doyle, who was injured for much of the campaign. Tommy Booth was a more than adequate deputy, though. City finished fourth with just three wins in the final thirteen games costing a repeat finish of the previous season at the least. Things were changing at Maine Road, however, and part way through the 1978–79 campaign, Malcolm Allison returned as first-team coach.

Allison didn't see eye to eye with many of the senior established stars, and within a six-week period, Asa Hartford, Peter Barnes, Gary Owen, Colin Bell and Dave Watson had all played their last game for City. It was a foolish move by Allison, who undoubtedly instigated the departure of at least four of those players (Bell retired), and it ripped the very heart out of the team that Tony Book had been patiently building for the past five years.

Watson decided to seek his fortune in Germany with Werder Bremen before having spells with Derby and Southampton. He won 65 England caps during his career and was very much from the old school of defending – hit them hard and keep it simple. City haven't had anyone quite like Dave Watson since.

HALF-TIME CHAT

THE ANTI-CROWD IDOLS

There have been a large number of players who didn't cut the mustard with City fans. Sometimes it was because they weren't particularly good, but at other times, it was much harder to fathom why they became a target for frustration and – sometimes worse – a focus for the dreaded 'boo boys'.

Every club has supporters like this and all real fans will agree they are detrimental to the team, but sometimes these things happen and a group of supporters will just want a player out of their club. That's how it works, and it's not always in the best interests of all concerned.

Take Ian Bowyer, for instance. He was a young lad making his way in the game who never quite managed to win over the fans. His confidence suffered, and it became only a matter of time before he had to move to further his career while he still could. Yet 17 goals in 57 starts is a fair record for a midfielder – in fact, it's a bloody good record. Bowyer finally ended his personal nightmare by joining Orient in 1971, and he would later become one of Brian Clough's most important players, shining for Nottingham Forest during their all-conquering period of the late '70s.

Other cases are more obvious. Mark Ward got off to a bad start at City simply because he'd been swapped for Kippax hero Ian Bishop. He was an undeserving focus of dissent among some City fans, and he never quite managed to shake the monkey off his back.

And how must Rick Holden have felt with all but a few in the ground feeling he wasn't quite up to the job. He was slow, and this was sometimes misinterpreted as lazy, but he was also a tremendous crosser.

Adrian Heath was often seen as the reason Clive Allen wasn't in the team and when a crowd favourite is axed, the replacement needs to be already well-liked or they are skating on thin ice from the start. Kevin Bond knows that to be true as he took over Nicky Reid's position in the early '80s.

Some, however, battle on through and win respect and, in rare cases, adulation. Trevor Morley was considered a dodgy buy for a while, but he never gave in, and the City fans came to admire his attitude and he ended up becoming something of a cult hero. Even Joe Corrigan went through a spell when he was targeted for criticism by some sections of the Maine Road crowd.

Steve Daley never won the fans over, but his cost was so high (at a then record British transfer fee of £1.4 million) that he could never hope to be value for money. The weight on his shoulders proved too much of a burden, and he was, by all accounts, a shadow of the player he was at Wolves.

If all this paints a poor picture of the fans, it certainly isn't meant to. Nobody has stuck by a club like the hordes of loyal supporters who have been with the Blues through thick and thin, but then nobody could deny the players mentioned above had a tough time during their spells with City. People are entitled to their opinion if they pay money at the gate. Every club is the same and many are far worse. There just seems to be a time when somebody doesn't gel or his face doesn't fit. It's life, and it happens in every profession. Sometimes all that's missing is an explanation as to why – but then again, it can't be ruled out that in some cases the individual concerned was just bobbins.

20–11

EVER-PRESENTS

NO. 20: FLOORED GENIUS – PAUL LAKE

SIGNED: 1985 from Blue Star

LEFT: 1993 Retired

CROWD IDOL RATING: * * * *

NICKNAME: 'Lakey'

APPEARANCES: 130 (+4 as sub)

GOALS: 11

SPECIALITY: Versatility

GREAT GOAL: Scoring on his home debut v. Luton Town, 1987

UNFORGETTABLE MOMENT: Setting up the fourth goal in the 5–1 win over United (1989)

FLAWS: Injuries by the bucket load

Lakey's story: Ask any Manchester City fan who saw Paul Lake play and they will tell you he was destined for great things and certainly had a rosy England future ahead of him. At a time when Mike Atherton was earning the nickname 'FEC' (Future England Captain) in cricket, Lake could easily have done the same in football. His was a rare talent – a complete footballer that could play anywhere and was good at whatever he did. He was destined to be a Maine Road legend until injury cut him down at a criminally young age.

Born in Denton, Lake was spotted playing for local side Blue Star and snapped up on schoolboy forms in 1985. In his first season with City's youth team, he helped them win the prestigious FA Youth Cup, scoring four goals along the way to the final, which City won, beating Manchester United 3–1 over two legs. It was a fairy-tale start for a youngster who was already a die-hard Blue and had dreamed of playing in front of the Kippax since he was a kid. The 1985–86 youth team, run by

Paul Lake – a shining light that glowed all too briefly

Glyn Pardoe and Tony Book, was full of talent and quality, but Paul Lake was arguably the cream of the crop.

Smooth as a Rolls-Royce in midfield, and commanding and elegantly powerful in defence, he could supplement attacks and score goals. He was also an excellent passer, solid tackler and first class in the air. In short, he had it all. At school he was no doubt the lad that could play any sport and be head and shoulders above everyone else – every school has one.

Blues manager Jimmy Frizzell decided to blood his precocious talent against Wimbledon at Plough Lane, and Lake, aged 19, more than held his own as City held the Crazy Gang to a 0–0 draw. He played in the following game – another draw, this time at Norwich – and then marked his home debut with a goal in the 1–1 draw with Luton. Those would be his only appearances that season, but he'd already made his mark.

During the summer, Frizzell left and Mel Machin took over. Machin was a good coach with a reputation for giving youngsters a chance, and his arrival at City was timed to perfection as the majority of the successful FA Youth Cup team of 1986 were ready for first-team football. Lake didn't feature in Machin's first four games, but after that, he only missed games if he was unfit.

Machin was quick to see Lake's value and versatility, playing him in nine different numbered shirts throughout the campaign. The fans had taken to Lake, and it wasn't long before comparisons to a young Colin Bell were made. Lake also won the first of five England Under-21 caps in 1988.

In season 1988–89, Lake largely played at right-back or in midfield and was inspirational as the Blues charged towards promotion. But there was one moment when, for a few minutes, thousands of City fans wondered whether they were witnessing the death of this up-and-coming youngster. During the visit of Leicester City in March 1989, Lake went up for a header and clashed heads with a Foxes player, crashing to the ground in a limp heap. What had seemed a routine head injury soon developed into something far more serious as the players around Lake suddenly began panicking and waving over the club doctor. Lake was convulsing and his legs were twitching as he slowly suffocated, having swallowed his tongue. Fortunately, the doctor freed his air passage and effectively saved his life. The atmosphere fell flat and quiet, even though City ran out 4–2 winners, as everyone wondered what had become of the youngster.

He missed one game as a precaution, but it was just the start of the then 21 year old's wretched luck. Machin was sacked midway through the following season, but not before he presided over a majestic 5–1 win against Manchester United. Lake, one of six Mancunians in the City side that day, savoured every moment and celebrated as any other fan would – ecstatically. He had also set up two goals for good measure. Howard Kendall came in and, realising what a gem he had, played Lake whenever he was available.

He even won an England B cap in 1990 and was mentioned as a possible for Italia '90, although ultimately he was forced to watch the World Cup on TV like the rest of the nation – even though every Blue knew he was ready for a bigger stage by that point.

Three matches into the following campaign and Lake's career was in tatters. During a home match with Aston Villa, Lake jumped with Tony Cascarino and fell awkwardly. What had seemed like a bump on the knee turned out to be a snapped cruciate, and he was ruled out for the rest of the season. Losing Lake meant Kendall needed another midfielder so he recalled the experienced Gary Megson, who did a steady job in his absence. However, Megson for Lake hardly excited the Blues' loyal following!

Fans wondered when Lake would return, but another season passed ominously without him playing. City finished fifth twice in the league during his absence, but the question being asked by many fans was where would the team have been with a fit Lake?

He underwent several operations but suggestions his career was over were whispered around Maine Road; whispered because nobody wanted to believe that a 23-year-old thoroughbred, who just might have been the future of Manchester City, could be finished because of such a nothing challenge.

Much like Colin Bell, one of his heroes, Lake painfully fought his way back to something like fitness, but this attempt would be his final comeback. Lake now accepts it was just his desire to play for the Blues again that was spurring him on. His knee was beyond repair and didn't feel right, yet his heart drove him on. When he made a block tackle during a pre-season friendly in Italy, he knew something was very wrong.

Yet he still managed to turn out for the first game of the 1992–93 season as the Blues took on QPR in Sky Sports' first-ever live *Monday Night Football*. As the fireworks and cheerleaders, part of the pre-match entertainment, left the pitch, Lake ran out at Maine Road for what would be his last appearance in a home game. From the start, he didn't look his old self – totally understandably – and was eventually replaced by Mike Sheron. However, player-boss Peter Reid selected him for the trip to Middlesbrough just two days later. It was football suicide for Lake, who was asking a hell of lot from his knee and perhaps should have been rested. Whether it would have made any difference at all is doubtful, but within minutes of the game at Ayresome Park kicking off Lake collapsed in agony. The look on the City players' faces said it all, and the normally mild-mannered Niall Quinn was sent off minutes after Lake was stretchered off, clearly frustrated and angry at the young midfielder's shattering setback.

Lake's career was over, but he wouldn't (or couldn't) give up, and City stood by him throughout several attempts to regain fitness, including a revolutionary transplant operation in the USA. All attempts failed, and Lake finally retired from the game. Although he was devastated, a huge weight of unfair expectation and hope had, perhaps, been lifted from his shoulders. In 1996, he returned for a deserved testimonial against United, who sent a full-strength team out of respect, and a crowd of 25,000 turned out to pay homage to a local hero.

The only certainty about Lake was that he was destined for greatness. How high he could have gone was quite literally up to him. Sadly, none of us will ever know.

NO. 19: FOREVER YOUNG – NEIL YOUNG

SIGNED: 1959 from Manchester Boys

LEFT: 1972 for Preston North End, £48,000

CROWD IDOL RATING: * * * *

NICKNAME: 'Nellie'

APPEARANCES: 413 (+3 as sub) .

GOALS: 108

SPECIALITY: Left-foot thunderbolts

GREAT GOAL: Without doubt his 1969 FA Cup-winning goal v. Leicester City

UNFORGETTABLE MOMENT: See above!

Nellie's tale: Neil Young was a Fallowfield lad, born just the other side of Platt Fields and within a Joe Corrigan kick of Maine Road. He signed in 1959 and rubbed shoulders with the likes of Denis Law, Billy McAdams, Joe Hayes and Bert Trautmann, though he didn't make his debut until late November 1961.

Manager Les McDowall gave the youngster his debut away to Aston Villa, and Young played in all the remaining twenty-four league games, scoring a healthy ten goals in return. In 1962–63, his first full season at senior level, he was part of the side that was relegated after a humiliating campaign in which 102 league goals were conceded. That included two 6–1 defeats to West Ham and an 8–1 opening day hammering by Wolves. It was a City-type learning curve where you either returned stronger or crumbled into dust and disappeared.

Young missed only five league games as the Blues, now under the reign of George Poyser, finished a disappointing sixth, and though he enjoyed his best goals tally yet the following season, it was even flatter at Maine Road when the fallen giants finished eleventh – the club's lowest finish for seventy-one years.

Joe Mercer was recruited to revive fortunes, and City stormed back to the top-flight as champions, with Young the top scorer. He possessed a lethal and cultured left foot, and his influence on the team was growing all the time. He could strike a ball sweetly from anywhere around the box, and when he caught hold of it, there was a fair chance he would bulge the net with an unstoppable drive.

Tall and graceful, Young was a bonus for Mercer, who had recruited Mike Summerbee to take over the No. 7 shirt and instead put Young in at No. 11. After a consolidating first 12 months back at the top, City took the title in 1968, and the gifted Young was imperious throughout the season, notching 21 goals in all competitions.

It was a dream come true for the kid who used to hang around Maine Road imagining himself inside the ground scoring goals for his heroes. In 1969, he emulated every schoolboy's dream by scoring the winner in an FA Cup final as City beat Leicester 1–0. Summerbee's precise cross fell to somewhere near the penalty spot and Young, now wearing No. 10, arrived bang on cue to wallop the ball home into the roof of the net. It was the stuff of fairy tales, and despite being left out of the 1970 League Cup final team almost a year later, he scored one and won a penalty as the Blues landed the European Cup-Winners' Cup trophy a few weeks later.

The only way was down from that point on for the man the Kippax lovingly nicknamed 'Nellie', and he made just twenty-four starts in 1970–71, scoring only once. Halfway through the next campaign, the Blues accepted £48,000 from Preston for his services. Young was the first real star to leave City following the glorious late '60s period – depending on how highly you regard Tony Coleman – and his contribution to the club should never be forgotten.

NO. 18: THE JINKING WINGER – PETER BARNES

SIGNED: 1972 from school, and 1987 from Manchester United, free

LEFT: 1979 for West Brom, £750,000, and 1988 for Hull City, free

CROWD IDOL RATING: * * * *

NICKNAME: 'Barnsey'

APPEARANCES: 149 (+12 as sub)

GOALS: 22

SPECIALITY: Touchline capers

GREAT GOAL: A dummy to die for then a superb chip v. Spurs, May 1977

UNFORGETTABLE MOMENT: Scoring the first goal in the 1976 League Cup final

FLAWS: Left the club too early – but, then again, he didn't seem to have much of a choice

Barnsey's tale: To a generation of kids that grew up in the '70s – this writer included – there was no finer sight than Peter Barnes running down the left flank for the Blues. He was perfect hero material for any youngster, and he was a crucial part of City's excellent mid-'70s team.

Tony Book had no hesitation in giving the teenager his league debut away to Burnley in October 1974. Yet he was patient with his precocious talent, blooding him in just three games in total that season before giving him his first sustained run part of the way through the following campaign.

With Rodney Marsh's days at City over, following an abject performance against Burnley, Book turned to Barnes to provide the team's creative spark on the flank. He played in twelve consecutive league games, and City remained unbeaten in every one bar the twelfth, when he was injured during a 1–0 defeat at home to Leeds, the first of three successive league defeats.

The dashing winger recovered from injury and took his place in the starting line-up safe in the knowledge that so long as he did the business on the pitch, the shirt was his. As City powered their way to the 1976 League Cup final, Barnes handled the more

Peter Barnes — patrolled the flanks of Maine Road and was a hero to many a youngster

than 100,000-strong Wembley crowd superbly. The nineteen year old opened the scoring for City with a clinical finish from close range against Newcastle as the Blues triumphed 2–1 to lift the trophy for the second time in six years. He also won the first of his nine England Under-21 caps that year, and the following year, he won his first full cap – thirteen more would follow.

The 1976–77 campaign was not a particularly memorable one for Barnes, who made just 16 starts, mainly due to injuries, but he returned to the side for the final push for the league title as City raced neck and neck with Liverpool to lift the most coveted prize in English football. With three games to go, City faced Spurs at Maine Road, and it was Barnes who tortured the Londoners, scoring a magnificent solo goal in a 5–0 win and having the rare accolade of chipping the great Pat Jennings to add to his already glowing CV.

Ultimately, the Scousers took the league by one point, and although nobody realised it at the time, the club began a slow but terminal descent into unorganised chaos that would last the best part of twenty years. There was still one more terrific season before the rot set in, and Barnes was magnificent as City finished fourth, finishing up with eight goals from his thirty-three league starts.

The fans loved Barnes for many reasons: the older generation had a soft spot for him because he was the son of '50s' hero Ken Barnes, whilst the younger generation idolised him because he was such an exciting player to watch, full of trickery, speed and intelligent wing play. Commentator Barry Davies seemed to think Barnes was England's answer to the Scottish flyer Jimmy 'Jinky' Johnstone, constantly describing his performances on the flank as 'jinking' – whatever that actually meant.

The player even promoted the Peter Barnes Trainer – a ball on a piece of elastic that you clipped to your shorts and was meant to improve ball skills. However, as anyone who ever owned one will surely confirm, it was a dangerous piece of kit, capable of making any young man talk permanently like Alan

Ball if they kicked it too hard. It doesn't take a genius to work out that if you kick a ball on a piece of elastic hard, it's apt to come back twice as fast and . . . well, use your imagination . . .

Barnes was to have one more season at Maine Road, but Malcolm Allison had replaced coach Bill Taylor by the New Year, and Big Mal wanted to completely rip up Tony Book's team and start afresh, which meant a whole host of established stars were shown the door at Maine Road, Barnes included.

He and his teammate and fellow youth team graduate Gary Owen, another crowd favourite, both joined West Brom during the summer of 1979 for a combined fee in excess of £1 million – Baggies boss Ron Atkinson couldn't believe his luck. The following season, both players inspired the Midlands team to a 4–0 win at The Hawthorns and a 3–1 win at Maine Road as if to prove to City what a terrible error they'd made in letting two home-grown stars leave when both clearly loved playing for the Blues.

Barnes went on to play for a number of other clubs, including Leeds United, but in 1987, eight years after he left the club, he was re-signed on a free from Manchester United.

It was a grave error of judgement all round, but boss Jimmy Frizzell took a chance on the ageing – and now portly – winger, who had only briefly been at Old Trafford. He played him for eight games towards the end of the Blues' ill-fated 1986–87 campaign, none of which City won, and they were relegated back to Division Two five games later.

Barnes left again, this time bound for sunny Hull, and he retired not long after. It was sad for many fans to see their idol return under such circumstances, especially when so many remembered his halcyon days when he was the best winger in the country.

NO. 17: THE STYLISH SCOUSER – IAN BISHOP

SIGNED: 1989 from Bournemouth, £700,000, and 1998 from West Ham, free

LEFT: 1989 for West Ham, swap involving Trevor Morley and Mark Ward, and 2000 for Miami Fusion, free

CROWD IDOL RATING: * * * *

NICKNAME: 'Bish'

APPEARANCES: 83 (+ 34 as sub)

GOALS: 7

MOMENT IN TIME: The diving header to put City 3–0 up against Manchester United in the famous 5–1 derby of 1989

GREAT GOAL: His piledriver against Leeds United in the FA Cup

SPECIALITY: Passing

NOT A LOT OF PEOPLE KNOW THAT: Howard Kendall ordered Bish to have his hair cut at both City and Everton – jealousy perhaps?

Bishop's story: You couldn't miss Ian Bishop when he played for Bournemouth. His stylish midfield play looked out of the ordinary when compared with the average journeymen around him, and his long flowing locks drew ironic wolf whistles from opposing fans. The first time he really came to the attention of City fans was when the Blues, needing a win to secure promotion during the 1988–89 campaign, raced into a 3–0 half-time lead against Bournemouth at Maine Road. The party began on the Kippax because even City couldn't throw this away . . . could they? Bishop played his part in ensuring they did, with Luther Blissett equalising from the spot in something like the 97th minute – so when anyone asks for explanations of the 'typical City' tag, this game pretty much sums it up.

Mel Machin liked what he had seen and snapped up the midfielder

Ian Bishop – his first stay summed up what being a crowd idol is all about

for £700,000 following City's last-gasp promotion clincher the following week at Bradford. Bishop jumped at the chance to move to Maine Road and was an instant hit with City fans, locking horns in one particular game with Paul Gascoigne – then in his pomp – and edging the battle with clever passing, dummies and the odd nutmeg. In fact, Bishop wasn't just popular, he was idolised by the City fans during his first spell, and he pulled the strings in the 5–1 win over United that year, scoring with a diving header and then playing an inch-perfect lofted ball that David White raced on to and crossed for Andy Hinchcliffe to make it five.

Bishop scored with another header the following week in a 3–1 win over Luton Town – bizarre considering heading just wasn't his forte at all. However, things soon went wrong for the Blues, and following a 6–0 loss at Derby, Machin was fired. Howard Kendall, who had previously had a spat with Bishop when he was an apprentice at Goodison Park for having hair that was too long – and who also subsequently released the player – took over and quickly signed dogged midfielders he felt would save City from the drop. Peter Reid and Alan Harper were signed and Gary Megson recalled – Bishop, all too predictably, was dropped. As Christmas approached, Kendall decided to bring in Mark Ward from West Ham, and to the City fans' dismay, Bishop was part of the exchange deal.

With the writing on the wall, he played his last game against Norwich. When substituted for the last time, he saluted the Maine Road faithful and left the pitch in tears. It was an unforgivable act by Kendall in the eyes of many fans, and he was never warmly received at the club again, just accepted. Bishop was afforded generous receptions on his return to Maine Road in the claret and blue of West Ham and he went on to become a real favourite at Upton Park. He was very much in the West Ham mindset of slick passing and attacking football. Meanwhile, the City fans watched Megson and Harper lumber around the midfield like geriatric dinosaurs – wholehearted, yes; pleasing to the eye, most certainly not.

Incredibly, the best part of an entire decade passed before Bishop returned to Maine Road. Joe Royle was by then in charge at City, and when Bishop was made available on a free transfer by the Hammers, who better, thought Royle, than Bishop to orchestrate his team, now in the nation's third tier, back to the upper echelons of English football?

The transfer was warmly received, and for many it was a treat to see 'Bish' back where he belonged. The trouble was, he was now at the wrong end of his career, and the years had taken the sharpness out of his play, although he could still pick a pass. The relationship with the fans wasn't the same – how could it be? But he was still a popular player – and a bloody good one, too. His guile and vision played a major part in City's dramatic return to the First Division, where he again played his part in a second successive promotion.

The Premiership was maybe asking too much, though, and he left for the USA to play for Miami Fusion, later returning to run a pub in Southport for a while. His last known whereabouts were coaching in the States. If only Kendall had never managed City, Bish would have probably been with the club for most of his career. Pity.

NO. 16: MAN MOUNTAIN – ANDY MORRISON

SIGNED: 1998 from Huddersfield Town, £80,000

LEFT: 2001 – out of contract

CROWD IDOL RATING: * * * *

NICKNAME: 'Mozzer'

APPEARANCES: 47 (+1 as sub)

GOALS: 5

SPECIALITY: Rousing his teammates and enjoying a good ruck with the opposition

CATCHPHRASE: 'Whomp! There it is!'

GREAT GOAL: 25-yard volley at Oldham Athletic

UNFORGETTABLE MOMENT: Lifting the play-off trophy at Wembley in 1999

FLAWS: Injured too often

Mozzer's tale: Few players have had quite the impact Andy Morrison did when he first arrived at City, initially on loan from Huddersfield Town. With an imposing physical presence, the strapping centre-half looked more like an army drill instructor, or perhaps a nightclub bouncer, than a professional footballer, but if anyone thought he'd be better suited to those particular roles, within a couple of appearances for the Blues those doubts had evaporated into thin air.

As the old saying goes, if you were in the trenches, you'd want somebody like Andy Morrison in there alongside you. For any centre-forward that was even slightly faint of heart, Morrison cut a menacing figure. Built like a brick outhouse with a shaved, flat-top hairstyle, he was straight out of a Vietnam War movie. Tough as old boots, he went in where it hurt, and when he hit players in the tackle, they stayed hit.

In the nicest possible way, he was an inspirational beast of a player.

He was also the perfect man to help resurrect an ailing City team who were floundering in Division Two, a ship without a captain. Joe Royle brought Morrison in on a month's loan, and his impact was nothing short of dramatic. He scored in both of his first two games for City – one a last-gasp winner against Colchester and the other a screamer at Oldham – and he galvanised a lightweight back four that had been soldiering on with young Nick Fenton at centre-back. In this dog-eat-dog division, youngsters like Fenton were something of a liability and often an easy mugging victim to some of the gnarly journeyman strikers lying in wait.

Andy Morrison – the big fella with
a heart to match – helped change
the club's destiny with an iron will and
determination to succeed

Royle moved quickly to seal a permanent move for Morrison, and at a cost of just £80,000, the Blues had at last acquired a genuine leader to take charge, halt the slide and resurrect their fading hopes of promotion. Mozzer hated slackers and was forever shouting, cajoling and organising the defence – in short, he was a natural captain.

City's form turned slowly but surely, and they lost just two of their final twenty-five games (both defeats at home) as they powered their way to the play-off decider against Gillingham. Morrison was injured early on at Wembley and had to be substituted, but he was able to collect the trophy at the end after the Blues triumphed on penalties – and boy did he enjoy it.

He was a good player, too, and far from the big daft centre-half he was, no doubt, often perceived to be by casual observers. He could pick 50-yard passes with a precision and weight that Glenn Hoddle would have been proud of and was dominant in the air. He was, however, the first to admit that his anger sometimes got the better of him, resulting in the occasional dust-up with the opposition.

The City fans loved him for it though. He was wholehearted and dedicated to the cause, and he was finally earning the recognition he deserved after many years in the lower leagues. Why it took him so long to climb the ladder is a mystery, but it's fair to say that many scouts looked at his appearance and build and thought him no more than a thug. More fool them.

City began the new season like a runaway train, and Morrison played his part to the full, but following a 2–1 win over Port Vale in October 2000, he picked up a nasty knee injury that ruled him out of the remainder of the campaign. For Mozzer, after finally finding a club he could make real progress with, it was a devastating blow that he understandably didn't take too well. He also missed the first half of the Blues' return to the Premiership, but was fit for the first game of the New Year.

It was a different Andy Morrison who returned, however, looking unusually hesitant and making the odd uncharacteristic mistake. He scored in his second comeback game, much to the delight of the ecstatic Maine Road crowd, but it was clear that his injury hadn't entirely cleared up and it was just his heart and desire that were pushing him on. City's 4–2 defeat at Liverpool in the FA Cup was to be his last game for the club, just six games into his return from injury. He then went on loan to Blackpool, Crystal Palace and Sheffield United in a bid to convince Royle that he could compete with new signings Steve Howey and Richard Dunne, but despite 14 games with other clubs he was never selected again and left City in the autumn of 2001.

A wonderful servant to the club, his enthusiasm and efforts have never been forgotten by the City fans, and he undoubtedly inspired a team heading for anonymity to win promotion in successive seasons and become the Premiership side they are today.

NO. 15: THE LITTLE DIAMOND – ASA HARTFORD

SIGNED: 1974 from West Brom, £250,000, and 1981 from Everton, £350,000

LEFT: 1979 for Nottingham Forest, £500,000, and 1984 for Fort Lauderdale, free

CROWD IDOL RATING: * * * *

NICKNAME: 'Rod Stewart'

APPEARANCES: 320 (+1 as sub)

GOALS: 36

SPECIALITY: Archetypal midfield general, organisation

SONG: 'Asa Hartford, Asa Hartford, la, la, la, la, la, la!'

GREAT GOAL: Neat finish during rare 3–1 Boxing Day win at Liverpool, 1981

UNFORGETTABLE MOMENT: Passing medical for City despite having hole in heart

Asa's tale: When young Scot Asa Hartford went for his medical prior to joining Leeds United, it looked as if he was set for a glorious career at Elland Road with a team who looked likely to dominate the '70s. But tests showed that Asa had a hole in his heart and the deal collapsed leaving both the player and Leeds boss Don Revie devastated. Hartford returned to The Hawthorns for a short while, and during this time, City manager Tony Book went along to see Asa in action. He'd had a more close-up view of the Clydebank-born schemer when City beat West Brom 2–1 in the 1970 League Cup final and was convinced that if there was a health problem, it didn't affect his football one iota. He opened discussions with the Baggies and brought the player to Maine Road for a series of medical tests – all of which showed that the heart problem was, in fact, not a problem.

Asa Hartford – the Scottish midfield general

Leeds' loss was City's gain, and the Blues paid £250,000 to Albion and, in doing so, conducted one of the best pieces of business in the club's history. Hartford was a midfield dynamo in every sense and became pivotal to Book's team, taking on the prized No. 10 shirt vacated by Francis Lee the season before. He slotted in perfectly alongside Colin Bell and Dennis Tueart initially, as Book rebuilt the ageing team that had won so many trophies just a few years before. He made his debut in a 4–0 win over West Ham and scored the winner in his second game against Spurs.

The following season, the midfield proved to be problematic for Book. Bell was lost to injury, Rodney Marsh was dropped and then transferred, while youngsters Peter Barnes, Gary Owen, Ged Keegan and Paul Power flitted in and out of the side. Hartford was the one constant in the team, his role as leader and creative force more important than ever, and he was at worst a second captain to Mike Doyle.

He took the added responsibility in his stride and ended the campaign as City's third top scorer in the league with nine goals, scoring five in four games during one spell. He was also influential in the Blues' path to the 1976 League Cup final, playing in all eight ties and picking up his first winner's medal.

Hartford's third season was arguably his best as he marshalled youngsters Power, Owen and Barnes into a formidable midfield that was ultimately only bettered by Liverpool, who won the league title over the Blues by a point.

The Kippax had taken to Hartford in a big way because he was a player who never gave any less than his all. His was an unusual mix of skill and aggression, and he was undoubtedly one of the best midfielders of his generation.

In his fourth season, City finished fourth and Asa was at the peak of his powers – so much so that when Argentina '78 began, many City fans followed the World Cup as honorary Scotland fans because Asa was playing (and Willie Donachie, of course). It's a fact that he is second only to Colin Bell when it comes to international caps won – 36 – while playing for City.

Malcolm Allison's ill-fated return to Maine Road, however, was to put a spanner in the works for Asa's City career, and the new coach was eager to rid the club of all its international stars and replace them with young, inexperienced players. Asa survived what would be his fifth season at the club, scoring vital goals in the UEFA Cup run – including one against AC Milan – but at the end of the 1978–79 season he was on his way to Nottingham Forest, where he famously stayed just a few weeks under Brian Clough before moving to Everton.

It's hard to understand why things didn't work out for Asa at Forest – perhaps it was a personality clash – but, then again, it was mystifying as to why the Blues had let such an asset go in the first place. Tony Book called Hartford 'my little diamond', and his transfer was a huge disappointment to what was now becoming a largely disgruntled City following.

After just a couple of years away, however, new manager John Bond re-signed Asa, who slotted back into the No. 10 shirt as if he'd never been away. It was a hugely popular move and proved that, as many of the other established stars who were swept out of the club by Allison in 1979 would probably admit, he'd never wanted to leave in the first place. He played 68 more league games for the Blues but was powerless to stop City from being relegated in 1983.

After almost a decade at Maine Road, he then left for a swan song in the North American Soccer League (NASL) with Fort Lauderdale. He would later return in 1995 as Alan Ball's assistant, managing the team in a caretaker role for a while and then running the reserve team for several years before finally leaving the Blues once again in the summer of 2005. A fantastic player, a good coach and a top man: no wonder everyone remembers Asa Hartford as a true City Crowd Idol.

NO. 14: WHITE LIGHTNING – DAVID WHITE

SIGNED: 1986 from Salford Boys

LEFT: 1994 for Leeds United, £2 million swap deal involving David Rocastle

CROWD IDOL RATING: * * * *

NICKNAME: 'Whitey'

APPEARANCES: 328 (+14 as sub)

GOALS: 96

SPECIALITY: Acceleration

SONG: 'Oh David White is ******* fast, oh David White is ******* fast!'

GREAT GOAL: A scorcher off the post and into the back of the net v. Aston Villa, 1991 – one of four he scored that evening in a 5–1 win

UNFORGETTABLE MOMENT: Scoring his third and City's tenth goal in the 10–1 win v. Huddersfield Town, 1987

Whitey's story: David White progressed from the 1986 FA Youth Cup-winning team that also spawned the likes of Andy Hinchcliffe, Ian Brightwell, Steve Redmond, Paul Lake and Paul Moulden. He made his league debut aged only 18, coming on as a sub in the 1–0 defeat at Luton. He played sporadically for the first team that season, finding the net only once in nineteen starts.

The following year, Mel Machin took over from Jimmy Frizzell, and White became a permanent fixture in the City team, playing in every game during the 1987–88 campaign and managing 13 goals. White was heavily involved in the incredible 10–1 demolition of Huddersfield Town, making a couple and scoring a hat-trick himself. Who could forget him racing through the Huddersfield defence in a one-on-one with the Terriers' keeper, rounding him and sliding the ball home for number ten?

It was his first really exhilarating performance for City. Having suffered with nerves during his first season and having managed just two goals in his first thirty-five appearances, it showed he was capable of destroying teams with his electric pace and finishing – so long as his confidence was high.

David White – fast, fast and more fast, as the Kippax used to sing

He missed only one game during the 1988–89 campaign, and it was his perfect cross at Bradford City on the final day of the season that Trevor Morley scored from to give City the point they needed for promotion. In addition, he earned the last of his six England Under-21 caps against Poland later that year and was by now a firm favourite on the Kippax.

For the second year running, White missed only one game

as City consolidated their return to Division One, and he was superb during the 5–1 hammering of Manchester United, tormenting the Reds' defence all afternoon and laying on Andy Hinchcliffe's unforgettable header for the fifth of the afternoon.

Machin was sacked in November 1988 with Howard Kendall taking over, and the new manager continued with White now leading the line rather than playing in his original role of winger. When Niall Quinn joined the club, however, the perfect strike partner White had craved had finally arrived, and their lethal partnership became the bedrock of City's impressive fifth-place finish – their highest final placing for thirteen years and one ahead of Manchester United. White and Quinn scored 36 league goals between them and ended the 1990–91 campaign under yet another new manager in Peter Reid.

Arguably, White's greatest ever performance for the Blues came towards the end of that season when he scored four cracking goals away to Aston Villa in a 5–1 victory. White was unstoppable during the game and showed skill, power and speed in an unforgettable one-man destruction of a Villa side who were no pushovers. White was at the very peak of his game and was rewarded with a couple of England B caps shortly after.

City finished fifth again the following year, and White enjoyed his best-ever goal tally of eighteen, with Quinn also notching a dozen. White was rewarded with a full England cap but was only given the one chance to impress during a defeat to Spain. There was one defining moment during his England debut when he was put through on goal, but he fluffed his shot – and his chances of more caps, too.

It was symptomatic of White's game in that he could frustrate and delight in equal measure. On his day, he was dynamite, but when his confidence was at a low ebb, his finishing could be poor.

For a time, though, defences simply couldn't handle the Blues' deadly Quinn–White partnership. With Quinn's deft flicks and headers and White's lightning pace and success ratio in front of goal, the 'jet-heeled' White, as he was often called, scored a further sixteen goals as City finished ninth in the inaugural Premiership season of 1992–93. However, when Reid was sacked after four games of the 1993–94 season, it signalled the beginning of the end for David White as a Manchester City player.

New boss Brian Horton gave him 13 starts before swapping him for Leeds United's David Rocastle in a deal valued at £2 million, leaving Ian Brightwell as the sole survivor of the 1986 FA Youth Cup-winning team. White, who scored 96 goals in his time with the Blues, eventually moved on to Sheffield United, but his happiest and most fruitful days were without doubt spent playing for City, his hometown club, for whom he was, at times, electrifying.

NO. 13: DER BOMBER – UWE RÖSLER

SIGNED: 1994 from Dynamo Dresden, £750,000

LEFT: 1998 for Kaiserslautern, free

CROWD IDOL RATING: * * * *

NICKNAME: 'Der Bomber'

APPEARANCES: 165 (+12 as sub)

GOALS: 64

SPECIALITY: Headers and emotional celebrations (plus the odd dying-swan routine!)

CATCHPHRASE: 'Bally, I hate you!'

GREAT GOAL: Lobbing Schmeichel at Old Trafford during an FA Cup tie

UNFORGETTABLE MOMENT: Coming on as sub and scoring against United at Maine Road, then running towards Alan Ball to give him a mouthful

FLAWS: Diving

Uwe's tale: When he arrived on loan to help City stave off relegation, he had a German mullet haircut and looked like he might last a couple of weeks before returning whence he came. But Uwe Rösler was made of much sterner stuff, and he would go on to be the second most popular German player in the club's history – after Bert Trautmann, who made 545 appearances for City between 1949 and 1964. OK, there have only been a handful, but Uwe won the hearts of enough Blues to be one of the biggest crowd favourites of recent times.

He made his debut in a 1–1 draw at QPR, and within the next couple of weeks, Paul Walsh and Peter Beagrie also arrived at Maine Road. They proved to be inspired signings by Brian Horton, and the ten goals that this trio shared between them in

Uwe Rösler – the incredibly popular German
forward, here telling Alan Ball where to get off

the final eight games of the season secured the Blues' top-flight status for at least another year.

Rösler was signed on a permanent deal for £750,000, and the following season, he formed part of a terrific forward line that included Beagrie, Walsh, Niall Quinn and Nicky Summerbee. Indeed, Rösler's form meant Quinn had to make do with the bench on a number of occasions. Manager Brian Horton had an embarrassment of riches up front, and the football was open and entertaining, Rösler feasting off two of the best crossers in the game in the form of Beags and Buzzer. Injury kept him out for several games, but, along with compatriot Maurizio Gaudino, he enjoyed a terrific second half of the campaign, scoring four goals in one game against Notts County, and ended the season with twenty-two goals.

T-shirts appeared with 'Uwe's Grandad Bombed Old Trafford', and he forged a fantastic player–fan relationship. However, when Horton was sacked, things began to turn sour for Rösler. Though he played all but one of the matches in the first half of the 1995–96 season, towards the end of the campaign he was dropped in favour of Nigel Clough and new signing Mikhail Kavelashvili – a move that enraged the passionate striker – and when he clambered off the bench to score a wonderful equalising goal against Manchester United at Maine Road, instead of celebrating an obviously joyous moment, he pushed his teammates away as he ran towards Alan Ball, gesturing at the name on the back of his shirt. This would be another nail in Ball's coffin. The manager kept the fuming German on the bench for the trip to Wimbledon – a game City had to win, but lost 3–0. Quite how Ball could ignore somebody whose passion to play burned so fiercely is a mystery, but it was just one of many under his reign.

Rösler was reinstated for the last three games, scoring the winner against Sheffield Wednesday and converting a penalty against Liverpool on the final day of the season, but it wasn't enough, and the Blues were relegated.

Within two games of the 1996–97 campaign, Ball was sacked and Rösler's nemesis had gone. Rösler played all but three of the games during that season, scoring sixteen goals and forging a wonderful understanding with Gio Kinkladze. He played the majority of games but only found the net on seven occasions, and three games before the end of the season, Rösler made his final appearance for the club when he came on as sub at Middlesbrough.

Having scored 64 goals in 177 games for the Blues, he returned to Germany to play for Kaiserslautern in the Bundesliga and also got to play Champions League football for a while. He would later play for TB Berlin, Southampton and West Brom, though he found the net just twice in thirty-four games back in England.

Uwe Rösler was made for City, and it didn't quite happen for him at any other club – the fans loved him, he felt at home and he had the right players around him (Beagrie, Walsh, Quinn, Kinky).

He moved to Norway and played for Lillestrøm, but in April 2003 was diagnosed with chest cancer, having suffered a number of coughing fits whilst with the Scandinavian outfit. For a time things didn't look good for him, but, in true Rösler style, he beat the illness by showing the same kind of fight and passion for life as he had done while wearing the sky blue of Manchester City.

After being given the all clear, he returned to Lillestrøm and was eventually rewarded by being made manager of the club. Rösler said at the time he was poorly that the hundreds of get well messages and cards he received from City fans gave him the strength to pull through. He has returned to see City play in the new stadium and received a tremendous welcome from the Blues' support – after all, he was coming home, wasn't he?

NO. 12: THE AFRICAN KING – ALI BENARBIA

SIGNED: 2001 over lunch (see below)!

LEFT: 2003 for Al-Rayyan

CROWD IDOL RATING: * * * *

NICKNAME: 'Ali B'

APPEARANCES: 66 (+12 as sub)

GOALS: 11

MOMENT IN TIME: His display away to Sheffield Wednesday, 2001

SPECIALITY: Eye-of-the-needle passing

NOT A LOT OF PEOPLE KNOW THAT: City signed Djamel Belmadi and Yasser Hussein on Ali's recommendation.

Ali's story: Nobody knew who he was – that's the bottom line of what would become an amazing addition to City's promotion-chasing squad. When Algerian playmaker Ali Benarbia signed for City in September 2001, it's safe to assume that, apart from the odd world-football anorak, he was a completely unknown quantity. He was almost 33 and had been on trial with Sunderland after spending his entire career in France, and if he'd been any good, we'd have known, right? Well, that was the general consensus. Credit where it's due, Kevin Keegan pulled off a master stroke when he invited Ali to lunch at the club's Carrington HQ. He'd heard that his invited guest had not been happy about the lack of respect Sunderland had shown him during his brief trial, when it's believed Peter Reid insisted he watch the player train a few times before making a decision on whether or not he'd offer Ali a deal. But Ali wasn't happy with that at all – with his reputation, he probably felt he'd been doing the Black Cats a favour speaking to them.

He left the North East, never to return, and as he had a

friend at City who shared the same agent (Alioune Toure), he thought it would be nice to stop by and meet the great Keegan in person. Over what has now become an infamous salmon lunch, Keegan told Ali everything he wanted to hear, and he was as good as signed up before he left for his plane home.

Like Georgi Kinkladze and Eyal Berkovic before him, it took Ali about ten minutes to bewitch a packed Maine Road on his debut (against Birmingham City), and by the end of his first game, the man people knew nothing of was just about the only thing supporters wanted to talk about.

The main question was how come nobody in England knew anything about him? Benarbia had it all – skill, vision and a

Ali Benarbia – pure genius from the Algerian magician

wonderful football brain. He may have been at the wrong end of his career, but City fans knew they were in the presence of a genius from the first time they saw him to his final game just shy of two years later.

Along with Israeli magician Berkovic, City perhaps had one of the best midfields in the country – including the Premiership, where City were hoping to return to before long. First Division defences simply couldn't handle Benarbia, who was physically strong on the ball and couldn't be bullied out of a game the way Berkovic sometimes could. He inspired the team to such heights that the Blues were a joy to watch, and the 2001–02 campaign was one of the most enjoyable for perhaps 30 years.

City won the league at a canter, finishing comfortably ahead of the chasing pack and also scoring a record number of league goals. Benarbia's influence cannot be underestimated, and his vision created innumerable chances for the likes of Shaun Goater, Darren Huckerby and Paulo Wanchope – so many, in fact, that Wanchope said, 'He finds you when you can't find yourself!'

Many wondered if he'd be able to cut it in the Premiership, and after winning the club's 2002 Player of the Year award by a landslide, his appearances became less frequent in the top division. Ali's influence seemed a little less while his midfield partner Berkovic excelled, but age and tiring legs seemed to be the reason – Ali was 34 and the fast pace of the Premiership appeared to be jading him at times, though he was never less than inventive and bright.

It was clear that, despite another year on his contract, Benarbia wasn't entirely happy with his lot as he completed his second season at Maine Road, and the man who made thousands of grown men stand up and bow in homage every time he went near the corner flags decided to call time on his career with the Blues after a competitive pre-season friendly at Mansfield Town. With the career Ali had enjoyed, it was understandable he didn't want to be remembered as a bit-part player in his final year.

It was a huge blow to Keegan, who hadn't seen it coming. He never replaced Ali and shortly after fell out with Berkovic, thus going from having two of the most gifted individuals in his midfield, to none. City almost went down that season, but Ali did return for the inaugural City of Manchester game against Barcelona and was welcomed as a hero. People would say, 'If only we'd had him six years earlier.' If only indeed!

Because he had the kind of skill seen only once in a blue moon, those who saw him play will always fondly remember Ali. When once asked by a journalist if he'd ever had the kind of adulation he was getting at City anywhere else, he replied, 'Everywhere I go.' He was, to quote a Guinness advert, 'Pure genius'.

NO. 11: THE BIG IRISHMAN – NIALL QUINN

SIGNED: 1990 from Arsenal, £800,000
LEFT: 1996 for Sunderland, £1.3 million
CROWD IDOL RATING: * * * *
NICKNAME: 'Quinny'
APPEARANCES: 219 (+25 as sub)
GOALS: 77
MOMENT IN TIME: Penalty save v. Derby
SPECIALITY: Cultured hold-up play and exquisite control
SONG: 'Niall Quinn's disco pants are the best . . .'

Niall's story: Few thought that much of Niall Quinn's signing in March 1990. The twenty-three-year-old striker had spent seven years with Arsenal but had never really established himself in the first team at Highbury, and, at £800,000, his signing was something of a gamble. He would also be one of Howard Kendall's last signings as City manager before he went off to re-ignite his love affair with Everton.

But Quinn made an impressive debut against Chelsea and scored a vital equaliser, too, ensuring he'd bought some time with the doubters. It would be another six games before Quinn tasted his first defeat with his new club, and by then, City were well and truly clear of the relegation trapdoor. Quinn scored a couple of crucial goals in those games, and he was already proving to be a popular figure among the supporters.

It wasn't until the completion of his first full season at Maine Road, however, that Blues followers and the football world in general realised just how good a player Niall Quinn actually was. He formed a blossoming partnership with David White, and the mix of aerial dominance and White's lightning speed vaulted City to their highest top-flight finish in more than a decade.

In season 1990–91, Quinn became the club's talisman with several memorable performances in various games. His perfect hat-trick at Crystal Palace (one with his left, one with his

Niall Quinn — much-loved striker once described as a 'giraffe on roller-skates'!

right and a header) proved his credentials yet further, but it was during the home clash with Derby County that Big Niall's status reached that of a deity. He'd already scored in the game, but when Dean Saunders was hauled down by Tony Coton in the box, Coton was sent off and Quinn took over in goal. Quinn, unknown to Saunders, was a former Gaelic footballer and more than useful between the sticks, and as the kick was struck, he guessed right and saved the penalty.

It was an unforgettable moment and the fact that City went

on and won 2–1 made it all the sweeter. The Quinn–White partnership yielded fifteen goals in the final eight games of the campaign, Quinn scoring eight of them, and in the final game at home to Sunderland, the Blues knew that they had the opportunity of finishing higher than United for the first time in thirteen years. Despite falling behind to the Black Cats, who were being backed by 10,000 travelling fans, all of whom knew that defeat would certainly condemn them to relegation, Quinn bagged a brace and White the winner as City won 3–2 and took fifth position in the final table, one ahead of the Reds.

In 1991–92, City finished fifth again, and Quinn was in the form of his life. White, too, had blossomed into something close to the finished article thanks to the Quinn effect and was prolific throughout the campaign, resulting in a call-up to the England squad.

Peter Reid moved on in 1994, and Brian Horton took his place. He decided his forward line needed freshening up and brought in Peter Beagrie, Uwe Rösler and Paul Walsh and played with two wingers. Some felt Quinn might be squeezed out, especially as he was sub for six of the first seven games, but the Blues began to flourish under Horton and Quinn played his part in the bounty of goals that flowed, particularly at Maine Road, where twenty-seven goals were scored in the first nine games of the season.

The team's form could not be maintained into the second part of the campaign, however, and at the end of the season, Horton was sacked. Alan Ball came in and again Quinn found himself on the bench at the start of the new term, but, once again, he fought his way back into the team without complaining in the interim. He was a model professional who had so much more to his game than being a target man. In fact, his height often masked his deft touch and excellent control. His exquisite one-two with Georgi Kinkladze against Aston Villa, resulting in a last-minute winner, illustrated that point perfectly.

City were relegated after Ball's first season in charge, and, during the summer, it was made clear to Quinn that he was no longer wanted at Maine Road – this despite his declaration that he was more than happy to stay and help the Blues win back their Premiership status. The problem seemed to be down to finances, but as Quinn was squeezed out of a club he would have happily ended his career with, it left a sour taste in his mouth.

Would City have won back promotion with Quinn in the team? We'll never know for sure, but it would have been far more likely. He instead headed off to Sunderland, becoming a legendary figure there, too, and striking up a very similar partnership to the one he enjoyed with David White at City, this time with Kevin Phillips.

When his testimonial was played to a full house of 40,000 at the Stadium of Light, he donated the £1 million gate receipts to charity – an unprecedented act of generosity and a slap in the face to those in the game who cannot see past their next hefty wage packet.

Niall Quinn really was in his own league and will always be fondly remembered by City fans.

10–1

FIRST NAMES ON
THE TEAM SHEET

NO.10: POCKET DYNAMO – SHAUN WRIGHT-PHILLIPS

SIGNED: 1998, following release from Nottingham Forest

LEFT: 2005 for Chelsea, £21 million

CROWD IDOL RATING: * * * *

NICKNAME: 'Wrighty'

APPEARANCES: 151 (+31 as sub)

GOALS: 31

MOMENT IN TIME: His spectacular strike against United in the 2004 Manchester derby to make it 4–1 to City

SPECIALITY: Dribbles, long-range shots and tackling – pretty much everything

SONG: 'Shauny Wright-Wright-Wright!'

NOT A LOT OF PEOPLE KNOW THAT: When he was signed from Nottingham Forest along with his younger brother Bradley, it was Brad the Forest scout believed would prove to be the bigger talent of the two

Shaun's story: It's now the stuff of legends that Nottingham Forest rejected Shaun Wright-Phillips for being 'too small'. City snapped up the young midfielder along with his kid brother Bradley and began to groom the pair for life at the academy.

Joe Royle returned to the club in 1998, and after his first training session at Platt Lane, he commented to the academy staff that 'the little fella was terrific' – Shaun had already caught the manager's eye aged 16.

It was Royle who drip-fed Shaun into his team, giving him the odd outing here and there, often as sub, before bringing him more and more into the first-team picture. It was clear he was a special talent, and when Royle was sacked in May 2001, Kevin Keegan said that he thought Shaun would one day play

Shaun Wright-Phillips – might have made the top three
had he not left for the bright lights of London

for England – and whether you view that as a prophecy or stating the obvious, he made sure Wright-Phillips was a regular fixture in his team from day one.

In fact, he was arguably the first name on the team sheet with his infectious enthusiasm providing a vital spark to Keegan's already talented, attack-minded side. Having made a large number of starts without scoring, it was typical that Shaun would finally find the net away from Maine Road, but he went one better than that by scoring in a game where, officially, there were no City fans at all. The match was against Millwall, who had banned any travelling support in response to City's decision to ban Millwall fans from Maine Road.

Shaun's goal that night was a cracker, and after that, he only ever seemed to score spectacular goals – and plenty of them.

The fans adored him for his never-say-die attitude and, of course, because he was a fantastic footballer who could lift the crowd with his own brand of genius. Wrighty was never one to lie on the floor injured after a challenge – he'd get up, hobble around and then play on. It wasn't his style (unlike some players at his new club!). On one occasion, his dad, Arsenal and England legend Ian Wright, watched a replay during a live match of a horrific challenge on his son where his knee almost bent inwards and said, 'Oh, he'll be OK. His legs are made of rubber!'

By the 2002–03 season, Shaun Wright-Phillips was perhaps the most important player in the City team. The following year he virtually *was* the City team. He was the driving force and creative outlet for the majority of attacks and he plundered goals from all angles and distances, but more often than not, they were 25-yard-plus sizzlers. It was no surprise to the City faithful that when he finally made his England debut – in a match against Ukraine – he marked it with a trademark run and low drive to score on his first appearance.

Unfortunately, that alerted the Stamford Bridge and Highbury vultures who began to openly declare how Shaun might fit into their team. In a stunning lack of respect for the Blues, Arsène Wenger impatiently urged Chelsea to make a bid because it was frustrating his transfer plans. This is the man who complains when Barcelona or Real Madrid sniff around Thierry Henry.

Worse still were Chelsea's whispers through the media, all, one assumes, designed to unsettle the player. Of course, they would deny such mind games, but the rumours went on too long to be mere speculation. It all seemed to be part of a grand design, and it would ultimately work like a charm.

Comically, Spurs were the first to bid hard cash – a joke offer of around £7 million that had City fans rolling in the aisles. Unfortunately, it was just the beginning. Wright-Phillips' stock continued to rise with stunning goals against Arsenal, Aston Villa, Southampton and numerous other efforts that proved he was the hottest young talent around.

With the rumours refusing to go away, he signed a new four-year deal at the start of the 2004–05 season and stated he would be happy if he never left the club. He played his part to the full but didn't quite sparkle as he had in previous years – a fact confirmed by his failure to win the City supporters' Player of the Year award that he had waltzed off with with such ease in previous years.

During the summer, the transfer saga continued, and it became a case of not if but when Chelsea would come in with an offer. They left it until the eve of the 2005–06 season to bid £20 million – a bid that was rejected by the Blues. The player backed this decision, claiming that he wanted to remain with City. But the next day, prior to a friendly at Macclesfield, he pulled out of the game feeling unwell, and it was around that time he informed chairman John Wardle he wanted to speak to Chelsea. From that moment on, he was on his way. An increased bid of £21 million was accepted, and he signed in time to join Chelsea's tour of America.

To the supporters, it was a bittersweet pill. Many felt betrayed, others understood the lure of Champions League football, but almost all agreed he should have given City one more season before he, for want of a better phrase, cashed in. As far as City were concerned, they'd done right by the player and the supporters, despite crippling debts, and had Shaun wanted to stay, that would have been that. What a pity things should end the way they did, with a somewhat sour taste to the whole affair. The likeable kid from London, rejected for being too small yet salvaged from the scrapheap by City and nurtured into one of Europe's most exciting players, had gone to rub shoulders with some of the cream of world football.

Yet he spent much of his first season on the bench and many wondered what his chances of keeping his England place were. Had he remained a City player, the question would surely have never been raised, but as the 2005–06 season entered the final straight, Wright-Phillips was playing on a regular basis for Chelsea – and playing very well – with the popular opinion being that he would make the final cut for the 2006 World Cup finals in Germany.

A terrific player and a genuine lad with it, his efforts in a City shirt will never be forgotten.

NO 9: KING OF ALL GEORDIES – DENNIS TUEART

SIGNED: 1974 from Sunderland, swap deal involving Mickey Horswill and Tony Towers worth £275,000, and 1980 from New York Cosmos, £150,000

LEFT: 1978 for New York Cosmos, £250,000, and 1983 for Stoke, free

CROWD IDOL RATING: * * * *

APPEARANCES: 265 (+10 as sub)

GOALS: 109

SPECIALITY: Overhead kicks!

SONG: 'Dennis Tueart King of all Geordies!'

GREAT GOAL: As if you didn't know!

UNFORGETTABLE MOMENT: Winning the League Cup final with *that* goal

FLAWS: Fiery temper – if that can be deemed a flaw

NOT A LOT OF PEOPLE KNOW THAT: As a superstition, he always followed No. 10 out of the tunnel and onto the pitch

Dennis's story: City snapped up the young Sunderland forward shortly after the Wearsiders' epic 1973 FA Cup final win over Leeds United. Mickey Horswill also joined the Blues on the same day, with Tony Towers moving to Roker Park as part of the deal.

Both new men made their debuts against Manchester United in front of 51,331 Maine Road fans and held their own in a 0–0 draw. Tueart was destined for great things with City, while Horswill would gradually fade away, some reckoned thanks to the influence of Rodney Marsh, who might or might not have been leading Horswill astray.

Tueart joined a City side going through major changes. After the Mercer–Allison reign came Johnny Hart, but ill health saw

Dennis Tueart – a hero to thousands of youngsters
and always exciting to watch

Ron Saunders take the hot-seat, and though he led the Blues to the 1974 League Cup final, Wolves triumphed 2–1 on the day. Tueart would be Saunders' last signing, and with the dressing room unhappy with the manager's regimental tenure, Tony Book took over for the last few games of the season when Saunders was sacked. Tueart played in the famous 1–0 win at Old Trafford on the final day of the season, with Denis Law's back heel securing the win and confirming United's relegation.

During his first full season, Tueart finished second top scorer with fourteen goals (Colin Bell scored eighteen) and also won two England caps. His feisty attacking style, backed up with skill, trickery and a strong desire to win, soon made him a major crowd favourite on the Kippax, and it became clear that he had found his spiritual home.

But it wasn't until 1975–76 that Dennis Tueart became a

household name in Manchester – and the rest of the country – and it was mainly for his exploits in the League Cup. He was a spree scorer and on numerous occasions when he scored one, he'd get at least another, or a hat-trick and even four in one match.

His first treble came in a second replay against Norwich at Stamford Bridge when City ran riot, 6–1. He was also scoring regularly in the league where, up to Christmas, City were among the leaders thanks to an 18-match unbeaten league and cup run.

Back in the League Cup, City lost Colin Bell during a 4–0 win over United, but despite this hammer blow, it was the tenacity of Tueart that inspired City to the final, where they would face Tueart's boyhood idols and hometown club, Newcastle United. During that game, he would score one of the club's most famous – if not *the* most famous – goals of all time, when he launched acrobatically to score a bicycle kick and win the League Cup for City. It was the type of goal you rarely saw in the English game at that time and the kind virtually nobody had managed before at Wembley.

If he had been a hero prior to that game, he had now moved up to the next level with the fans. The winning goal had been his eighth in the competition, underlining his influence on the route to glory. City, and Tueart, ended the season understandably a little emotionally spent, but for his 48 appearances, his return of 24 goals was excellent.

Tueart continued his fine form into the 1976–77 campaign, finishing second top scorer with eighteen goals from thirty-eight starts. He linked well with Brian Kidd and Joe Royle, and with Peter Barnes on one flank and Dennis on the other, it was no wonder that the Blues ran Liverpool so close for the title, missing out on being crowned league champions by a single point.

But Tueart was growing restless. There was a wanderlust inside him that was desperate to sample new horizons, and although he bagged twelve goals in seventeen games, including three hat-tricks during the first half of the 1977–78 season, after City went out to Arsenal in the quarter-finals of the League Cup he followed that ambition to the USA and signed for the New York Cosmos.

It was a deal that desperately disappointed City fans, who knew that the prospects of winning the league without Tueart were far slimmer. Following his departure, the Blues won just five of their last fifteen games and finished fourth. The lure of the NASL had proved too great for a flair player who wanted to sample the high life for a while. He actually joined Cosmos to cover the gap following Pelé's retirement the year before and played with some of the best players around at that time, including Franz Beckenbauer. Dennis scored ten goals in twenty games during his first season and won both the NASL Championship and the Soccer Bowl for Cosmos. The Soccer Bowl was played at the Giants Stadium in New York, and over 74,000 attendees watched Dennis score twice to secure a 3–1 win over Tampa Bay. Other former City players doing their stuff well in the US were Rodney Marsh and Trevor Francis, who both made the NASL All Star team in 1978.

Then, after two years away, he returned from the States to rejoin City, picking up where he'd left off and scoring vital goals in the last 11 games that helped the club avoid relegation. Injury meant he played exactly half the league games the following year and caused him to miss the first FA Cup final with Spurs, and although he was fit for the replay, John Bond kept the same side and left Tueart on the bench, preferring youngster Dave Bennett. He did come on for the final few minutes, but many believe he never forgave Bond for not playing him in the replay, which City lost 3–2.

He remained with the Blues for another two injury-plagued years, scoring fourteen league goals in forty-five starts before joining Stoke City in 1983. An extremely exciting player to watch, he was very much a Crowd Idol and a terrific servant of Manchester City, where, of course, he is now on the board with close links to the academy and the next generation of heroes.

NO. 8: LEE ONE PEN – FRANCIS LEE

SIGNED: 1967 from Bolton, £60,000

LEFT: 1973 for Derby County, £100,000

CROWD IDOL RATING: * * * *

NICKNAME: 'Franny'

APPEARANCES: 328 (+2 as sub)

GOALS: 148

SPECIALITY: Timing his dives to perfection – though he will deny this!

GREAT GOAL: His clipped goal and City's fourth to clinch the league title in 1968

UNFORGETTABLE MOMENT: His wonder goal for Derby County, on his return to Maine Road

FLAWS: Dodgy hairstyle!

Franny's story: Francis Lee was signed by Joe Mercer in 1967 in the hope that the £60,000 paid to Bolton would help the Blues land the First Division title. Lee wore the No. 7 shirt for his debut against Wolves, replacing Stan Bowles – who seemed to be coming into his own with four goals in four games – but Mercer preferred his new signing and dropped the home-grown Bowles.

Lee had a proven track record at Bolton, where he'd made his debut aged sixteen and had been playing first-team football for seven years. He'd also notched a very healthy 92 goals in 132 games for Wanderers. A very ambitious young man, he decided he wanted to leave Burnden Park and seek new horizons, but his transfer request was refused by the club. Lee, demonstrating an independence and determination to look after his own interests, promptly threatened to go on strike. The board relented, and when City made a firm bid, they reluctantly allowed Lee to join their near neighbours.

Lee was made for City, slotting in perfectly to the football and team ethic Mercer and Allison wanted in their side, and it wasn't too long before the management and supporters realised that the 23-year-old Westhoughton lad was the final piece of the jigsaw.

Lee, along with Colin Bell and Mike Summerbee, was part of a fearful trio for any defence to face – but throw in Neil Young and Tony Coleman and you have the club's best-ever forward line, full of quality, endeavour and sheer bloody-mindedness.

Lee, though physically short and stocky in appearance, was apt to give any defender a tough 90 minutes, no matter what their size. Feisty and fiery, he backed up guts with skill and intelligence and was soon a hero to thousands of City fans.

The Blues won eight and drew three of Lee's first eleven league games, and he scored eight goals as City sailed towards the summit of the table. Franny also volunteered to take penalties for the team and won most of them himself, though he was accused of diving in the box on many occasions – as if!

By the time City lifted the championship in May 1968, Lee had scored 16 in 31 games, and it was his strike at St James' Park on the final day of the season that effectively won the game and the title for Mercer's men.

Bell, Lee and Summerbee became known as the Holy Trinity, and the trio inspired more success the following year with a FA Cup final triumph over Leicester. Lee finished joint top scorer in the league, and a year later, it was a cup double for the Blues as they first lifted the League Cup and then the European Cup-Winners' Cup in 1970. Lee scored the decisive goal in Vienna (from the spot of course) to secure a 2–1 win and a first major European trophy for the club. That £60,000 was beginning to look like the bargain of the decade for City.

In what was a period of hard men in football, nobody bullied Franny Lee, who despite appearing to be carrying a few extra pounds was actually solid as a rock, and many a defender was bounced out of the way as he drove forward towards goal.

He finished top scorer again in 1970–71 and had his best-ever season for the club in 1971–72 when City almost won the league title – but 'almost' doesn't win medals or trophies, unfortunately. Lee scored an incredible 35 goals in 46 league and cup games and converted a record 15 penalties along the way.

Off the field, Lee's sharp business acumen ensured he was well on his way to becoming a millionaire while still a very young man. He was also an England regular, having played for his country in the World Cup finals in Mexico in 1970. In all, he scored ten goals in twenty-seven appearances for the national team.

In 1972–73, the unorthodox forward was becoming restless at Maine Road, and despite finishing joint top scorer for the Blues for the third time in six seasons (with a total of fourteen goals), the managerial upheavals that had seen Mercer moved unceremoniously 'upstairs' and then Allison quit after less than a year in charge left him wondering about his future with the club. Johnny Hart, Ron Saunders and then Tony Book all took turns in the management hot-seat, meaning that after having had just one manager for seven years, City had now had five in the space of two.

Lee, keen to secure a new deal with the Blues, wanted more money, and, with his track record, who could have argued against him? But his influence on the team was not all it had been, and he managed only ten goals in twenty-nine league games during the 1973–74 campaign, so when Derby County offered £100,000 for his services three days before the start of the new season, Tony Book didn't stand in his way.

It was a wonderful move for Lee and for the Rams, and just as he had been in his first season with City, Lee was inspirational as Derby went on to win the league championship in 1974–75. Lee, desperate to prove a point to the club he still loved, also scored a belter on his return to Maine Road in Derby colours. It was typical of the man, and the City fans who witnessed the goal didn't know whether to laugh or cry.

He played on for one more season at the Baseball Ground before retiring to concentrate on his thriving waste-paper business and successful racehorse stable. He would return to become chairman of City in the mid-'90s, although things didn't quite work out the way he'd hoped.

NO. 7: STINGING BEE – MIKE SUMMERBEE

SIGNED: 1965 from Swindon Town, £31,000
LEFT: 1975 for Burnley, £25,000
CROWD IDOL RATING: * * * *
NICKNAME: 'Buzzer'
APPEARANCES: 449 (+3 as sub)
GOALS: 68
SPECIALITY: Roughing up defenders
SONG: 'Sha-la-la-la Summerbee!'
GREAT GOAL: Championship decider v. Newcastle 1968
UNFORGETTABLE MOMENT: Pretending to blow his nose on the corner flag in front of the Stretford End

Buzzer's tale: Joe Mercer's decision to make Mike Summerbee his first signing as Manchester City manager prior to the 1965–66 season was arguably also one of his best. The Cheltenham-born winger arrived for just £31,000 from Swindon Town, upping his wage from £35 to £40!

The Swindon board had been reluctant to let their rising star leave the County Ground, but economics demanded they cash in and ultimately sell to the highest bidder. Fortunately for the Blues, that was Mercer, who had played football with Mike's dad George during the war. Summerbee proved an instant hit with the City fans and fitted perfectly into a side destined for promotion from the Second Division during his first campaign at Maine Road.

He played in all fifty-two games in league and cup competitions, scoring ten goals as the Blues returned to the top flight after a three-year hiatus. He added a new dimension to the team with his trickery and ability to get to the bye-line and whip over wonderful crosses. He was also one of the first wingers to actively go looking for a physical battle, tackling back and offering 50-50 balls in order to give the full-back an early taste of what was to come. Franny Lee said some years later it was a form of 'retaliating first'!

For many defenders, having a winger with attitude was something entirely new, and by the time the game was over, they knew they'd been in a battle. When Francis Lee arrived to supplement the attack, City were a formidable opposition for anyone and the championship was won with style in 1968, Summerbee's contribution being substantial. He played 50 games in all competitions, scoring 19 goals – a fantastic return.

But it wasn't just about the football. The fans loved 'Buzzer' because he was a real character who played the game in the right spirit, and he was a man's man. He was always prepared to enjoy himself – often with a deadpan look on his face – and would play to the crowd on occasion, throwing snowballs, sitting on the ball, blowing his nose on the corner flag – there were dozens of memorable moments. Then there was the time at Burnley when he placed a plastic cup on the ball before taking a corner. He loved winding up the opposition fans but took the return stick in good humour.

He was no clown, though, and he was totally professional in his attitude, flourishing in the bright lights of Manchester and ending up big pals with George Best. The pair even opened a boutique together at one point, and George was best man on Buzzer's wedding day.

Summerbee thoroughly enjoyed the life of a footballer and was a regular member of the first team for eight seasons, although he played more as an out-and-out winger as time went on, and, subsequently, his goal-scoring record began to suffer. His highlights were undoubtedly the league championship in 1968 – Buzzer scored the opening goal on the final day away to Newcastle to help secure the title – and when he laid on a perfect cross for Neil Young to hammer home the only goal of the 1969 FA Cup final.

He was also instrumental in the 2–1 League Cup final win over West Brom a year later but sustained a hairline fracture of the leg during the game which meant he missed the European Cup-Winners' Cup final just seven weeks later. Buzzer continued to give excellent service for many years at Maine Road, becoming skipper for the 1973–74 season and leading his team out at Wembley for the 1974 League Cup final against Wolves, though he had to settle for a runners-up medal on the day.

Like many City stars of the era and since, his haul of eight England caps was scant reward for his consistency and performances at club level, which merited at least three times that amount.

When Tony Book became manager in 1974, he had the difficult job of dismantling an ageing side full of former teammates, Summerbee included, and when Burnley lodged a bid of £25,000, Book allowed one of the most distinguished No. 7s in the club's history to leave.

He stayed for one year at Turf Moor and then left on a free transfer to Blackpool. A year later he moved to Stockport County and a year after that he became player-manager of the Edgeley Park outfit, resigning in October 1979. He never strayed too far from Maine Road, and after retiring from the game in 1981, he remained close to the club and has done ever since. Indeed, up to 2006 he was still involved with the commercial department and match-day programme.

It's not hard to understand why he was so popular – he had everything you would want in a winger plus much more. He was also a born winner. Outside of the game he was able to concentrate on his successful shirt-making business that could boast Sylvester Stallone and David Bowie among its customers. There was, however, one other diversion – Hollywood.

In 1980, the late Bobby Moore rang Summerbee and asked him if he fancied being a movie star. Never one to turn down a challenge, Summerbee signed up to be Syd Harmer in the film *Escape to Victory* that starred, amongst others, Pelé, Stallone and Michael Caine. That was Buzzer, always playing to an audience whether it was 10,000 or several million, and he was, of course, always entertaining to watch.

NO. 6: ENGLAND'S REAL NO. 1 – JOE CORRIGAN

SIGNED: 1966 from Sale FC

LEFT: 1983 for Seattle Sounders, £30,000

CROWD IDOL RATING: * * * *

NICKNAME: 'Big Joe'

APPEARANCES: 602 (+1 as sub)

GOALS: 0

SPECIALITY: Defying the odds

SONG: 'England, England's No. 1, England's, No. 1!'

GREAT SAVE: Away to Leeds United in the FA Cup when he turned in mid-air to push the ball over the bar

UNFORGETTABLE MOMENT: His emotional return with Brighton in 1983

Big Joe's tale: Joe Corrigan could easily have melted away from the professional scene and never made the grade in top-flight football had he not had the guts and determination to want to prove to the doubters – and initially they were legion – that they were wrong.

Signed in 1966, he was third-choice keeper behind Ken Mulhearn and Harry Dowd during the late '60s. He made his debut in a League Cup tie against Blackpool in 1967 but had to wait a further 18 months before making his league bow at Ipswich in March 1969. He made two further starts that season, but it wasn't until the 1969–70 season that he was given an extended run, keeping his first clean sheet in a 4–0 win at Roker Park. He became the number one No. 1 that year, but his confidence suffered and weight soared as the fans began to lose faith in his ability.

Against West Ham at Maine Road in March 1970, Corrigan punted the ball up field and then turned to walk back to the six-yard box. As he did, the ball flew over his shoulder and into the net, momentarily confusing the giant keeper before he realised somebody must have volleyed it on the full from the West Ham half. They had, and it was Ronnie Boyce who had damaged the youngster's confidence and reputation further – irreparably some reckoned. Joe never turned his back on a kick-out again.

He clung on to his place for the next four seasons, never making fewer than thirty starts in the league, before the Blues snapped up Motherwell's Keith MacRae to challenge for the No. 1 jersey. For the next two years, Joe played second fiddle to MacRae, but after the Scot was injured during a 1–0 defeat at Leicester, Corrigan was reinstated. Having worked tirelessly in training, he had lost a great deal of weight and looked slimmer and fitter than ever before.

The steely determination showed through in his performances, too. There was no way he was going to give his place up again, and he missed just one of the next two hundred and twenty-three league matches in an incredible run of appearances stretching over more than seven years. Eventually, with a ginger beard now down to his knees, MacRae quit Maine Road in search of a team without a superhuman as their goalkeeper.

For many, Joe Corrigan *was* Manchester City during the '70s. He was respected everywhere he went and was unbelievably consistent, never letting the club down and always being prepared to get hurt if it meant keeping the ball out of his net.

He struck up a wonderful relationship with the City fans who were full of respect and admiration for the way he'd turned his career around, and the sight of Joe running to Helen Turner in the North Stand to collect his lucky sprig of heather before a home game became a much-loved Maine Road tradition. Another well-known Corriganism was kneeling down on his

Joe Corrigan – a majestic last line of defence

haunches and facing the other way if the Blues were awarded a penalty. It was a superstition he continued with throughout his career.

Despite this, Joe was the third-choice England keeper with a succession of national bosses preferring Peter Shilton and Ray Clemence – both excellent keepers in their own right – but had he played at almost any other period since, he would have been England's No. 1 for perhaps a decade. As it was, his England B caps outnumbered his full caps by one (he played ten times for the unflatteringly named B team), and he was even chosen as an over-age player for the Under-21s in 1978, winning three caps.

After more than 600 games for City, he played his last match for the club in a 4–1 defeat to Swansea at the Vetch Field.

It was a disappointing note on which to leave the Blues, as he headed to America for pastures new. Quite how the club could sanction the sale of its rock and main influence amid a desperate relegation battle was never satisfactorily explained, but City were relegated two months after Joe's departure.

Would he have saved the club from the drop? Sadly, we'll never know the answer to that question, and it must be said that Alex Williams did his utmost to help the Blues preserve their First Division status and couldn't be faulted in his efforts. But Corrigan was a legendary figure, and it's mere folly to think that he would have made no difference whatsoever.

Things didn't work out in the USA with Seattle running out of money shortly after his arrival, and despite staying on for a short while as he tried to make the American Dream work out, Joe returned to England with Brighton and Hove Albion, who were now in the same division as City. Joe returned 'home' with the Seagulls in November 1983 to one of the most incredible receptions since Colin Bell's return from injury on Boxing Day 1977, with the applause sustained for several minutes as the Blues' loyal following finally got the chance to say 'thanks' to the big fella. City won 4–0 and Joe retired not too long after, becoming a goalkeeping coach at Liverpool for several years before going on to do the same job for West Bromwich Albion in 2006. A club legend and a Crowd Idol, in every sense, to City fans, he will always be England's No. 1.

NO. 5: MR BLUE BLOOD – MIKE DOYLE

SIGNED: 1962 from Stockport Boys
LEFT: 1978 for Stoke City, £50,000
CROWD IDOL RATING: * * * * *
NICKNAME: 'Doyley'
APPEARANCES: 563 (+7 as sub)
GOALS: 41
SPECIALITY: Winding Manchester United fans up
SONG: 'M-I, M-I-C, M-I-C-K, Mick Doyle!'
GREAT GOAL: 1970 League Cup final v. WBA
UNFORGETTABLE MOMENT: Lifting the League Cup as captain in 1976

Mike's tale: Mike Doyle was spotted playing for Stockport Boys and a local scout tipped off City's chief scout, Harry Godwin, that this was a young half-back definitely going places. Several clubs, including Wolves and Manchester United, were keen to take the Reddish youngster on, but Doyle came from a long line of Blues, and when he found out City were interested, there was only going to be one winner.

Doyle would go on to be one of the best players in the club's history, and he was certainly one of the most committed. In fact, there were many reasons Doyle was idolised by the City fans, but his very public hatred of Manchester United struck a particularly pleasing chord with the supporters. Doyle didn't just hate the Reds, he loathed them with a passion, and, throughout his career, he always found that little bit extra when the Manchester derby came around – so much so, he was once advised by a crank caller to stay away from Old Trafford or he'd be killed! Doyle played, City won – it was business as usual.

He made his debut away to Cardiff City in a 2–2 draw and did enough to impress manager George Poyser into giving him another five starts before the end of the season. Joe Mercer then took over, and he too was impressed by the young half-back, although new coach Malcolm Allison thought he'd make a useful emergency forward when required – and he was right: in one four-game spell he scored six goals as a stand-in striker. Doyle didn't mind where he played as long as he was wearing that pale-blue jersey. He always thought himself no different from the man on the terraces and claimed he was just a fan who was lucky enough to play for the club he loved.

Doyle was used only sparingly in 1966–67, with new signing Stan Horne preferred by Mercer, who'd had the player under him at Aston Villa. Towards the end of the season, however, Doyle reclaimed his No. 4 shirt and the next season was an integral part of the Blues winning the league title. An intelligent player with a good pass and pace about him, Doyle not playing for City soon became unthinkable. To illustrate the point, Doyle missed a dozen games between August 1967 and May 1971 and City lost nine and drew the other three in his absence – coincidence? Probably not.

As City lifted trophy after trophy, Doyle was there, giving his all with as much influence as a captain, but the fact Tony Book was *the* captain meant he was yet to lead his beloved Blues. Doyle played in every major final during the glory years and scored a vital equaliser in the 1970 League Cup final, as well as a crucial strike in the European Cup-Winners' Cup semi-final against Schalke 04 at Maine Road.

He took penalties, went in goal on numerous occasions and continually went on TV to tell everyone that City would 'stuff' United when the derby came around – and they generally did.

Mike Doyle – the fan off the terrace
that got to play for the club he loved

He once tried to throttle the late George Best when he broke Glyn Pardoe's leg, and he punched Leighton James during a game, and then, later the same evening, bumped into him in a Blackpool hotel and chased him out of the building.

Doyle was nobody's fool, and he was also a very talented footballer. He would have gone to Mexico in 1970 with England, but his wife was very ill and he told Sir Alf Ramsey he was unavailable – he only won six caps for his country but should have won many more.

Doyle never got along with Rodney Marsh and held the cockney striker in utter contempt. He represented everything he didn't like, and Doyle always thought Marsh's heart wasn't 100 per cent behind the cause.

When Marsh was stripped of the captaincy (that many felt

Doyle should have had anyway) in 1975, Tony Book gave the armband to Doyle, and he seemed to grow an extra foot in height. Leading Manchester City was an honour for him and another reason to give that little bit extra. He forged a fantastic centre-half partnership with Dave Watson, and there was no prouder man that Doyle when he lifted the League Cup in 1976.

He very nearly skippered his team to the league title the season after, just missing out to Liverpool by one point. If he'd managed it, his ambition would have been fulfilled. After picking up a couple of injuries towards the end of that season, he was also ruled out for much of the following campaign and later felt he was rushed back into playing too soon, causing him to ultimately miss more games.

It was a shock to the player and the legions of City fans, who loved having Mike Doyle around, when the club agreed to an offer of £50,000 from Stoke City. Doyle still felt he had another couple of good years left in him but accepted the move like a professional and finally severed his ties with his boyhood heroes for whom he'd made more than 500 appearances over a 16-year period.

On the night of his testimonial, around 10,000 fans attended. The reason for the numbers being so low? A bus strike on a midweek evening that cost him perhaps half of what the gate would have been. Mike's reaction? 'Just my bloody luck!' He claims to have used the apology letter from the bus drivers' shop steward as extra toilet paper! A legend, a working-class hero, a United-hater and someone not afraid to call a spade a spade – they don't make them like Mike Doyle anymore, that's for sure.

NO. 4: THE COCKNEY INTERLOPER –

RODNEY MARSH

SIGNED: 1972 from QPR, £200,000
LEFT: 1975 for Tampa Bay Rowdies
CROWD IDOL RATING: * * * * *
NICKNAME: 'Marshy'
APPEARANCES: 150 (+2 as sub)
GOALS: 47
SPECIALITY: Doing his own thing on the pitch, but it was always good to watch
GREAT GOAL: Ball juggling, turning and volleying home against Southampton
UNFORGETTABLE MOMENT: His comments to Sir Alf Ramsey (see below)
FLAWS: Too individual for the team of the time

Rodney's tale: Rodney Marsh cost City the 1971–72 title – let's get that old chestnut out of the way right from the start. Whether it's true is probably the most debated question in the club's history and most definitely impossible to prove either way – the fact is, his arrival may have disrupted the flow of the Blues at the time but, City being City, may have shot themselves in the foot all by themselves.

Marsh arrived from QPR for £200,000. He had a reputation for being a flair player, equally flamboyant in his private life as he was on the pitch, and his time at Maine Road was never dull.

You can almost picture the first day he arrived for training – a big flash car, jewellery and pop-star haircut. It was never going to go down well with the then northern home-grown lads in the City side, especially the likes of working-class hero Mike Doyle!

It was – surprise, surprise – Malcolm Allison's idea to sign Marsh. He felt he could be City's answer to George Best and put 10,000 on the gate, and, to be fair, that's exactly what happened with Marsh's debut against Chelsea seeing a crowd of 53,000 – 9,000 up on the previous home game with Arsenal. City beat Chelsea 1–0 and were still in an excellent position to take the title if they maintained their fine form, but a draw at Newcastle and shock defeats to Stoke and Southampton took the initiative away from the Blues and some blamed Marsh for that. Most of them, unfortunately, were his teammates.

It couldn't be argued that his style wasn't having an adverse effect on the quick, counter-attacking style that had become City's trademark. Whereas they used to get the ball wide to the likes of Tony Towers, who would whip the ball in quickly, Marsh would hold the ball, do a few tricks and generally slow things up. It was a huge gamble by Allison to pitch Marsh in at such a critical stage, one that ultimately backfired. There were even question marks about his fitness. Three wins in the last five games saw City finish fifth, and although that may have been respectable, it felt like they'd lost a cup final.

Marsh's first full season wasn't a roaring success, either, but the fans loved him all the same. He loved to play football and entertain, dribbling, juggling and generally doing tricks most players couldn't dream of, and nobody could deny he was great to watch. In fact, new boss Tony Book decided to make him captain, to see if the extra responsibility would enhance his all-round team play, and Marsh continued to beguile, bewitch and frustrate in almost equal measure during 1974–75 until the almost guaranteed fall-out with the management occurred. During a 0–0 draw with Burnley, Marsh's display was signalled out as particularly poor, and he never played for the Blues again.

It reinforced his critics' view that he was only in it for himself and that team ethic came a poor second to his own personal glory. Dropped and forced to train with the kids, his army of admirers began to kick up a fuss.

Fans protested and Tony Book received hate mail over his decision not to play Marsh, but Book felt the situation had become untenable. It was several months, however, before Marsh agreed a move to Tampa Bay Rowdies. He scored 11 goals in 31 games in his first season for the Rowdies before returning for a spell with Fulham (and Bobby Moore and George Best) in 1976–77. He then returned to Tampa, knocking in forty-eight goals in ninety-four games over a four-year period, and appeared in Soccer Bowl '79 (having missed out the previous year due to a leg infection). He was also named in two NASL All-Star teams, and following his retirement from playing, continued to coach in the States for a number of years.

Famously, Rodney was never one to keep his mouth shut when there was a chance of a smile or two, and while playing for England on one occasion, he was sitting in the changing rooms at half-time when the focus turned to him. Alf Ramsey warned him that he needed to work harder or he'd pull him off during the second half and Marsh replied, 'That's incredible, Alf. At QPR, we used to just get an orange.' He was never selected for the England team again.

Adored by the fans, colourful, flashy, hugely talented with a touch of arrogance but a real understanding of why football is the 'Beautiful Game', he was a true football genius and a unique character. There really was only one Rodney Marsh, and whether or not he did cost us the title way back when, thank God he played for City.

NO. 3: THE KING – COLIN BELL

SIGNED: 1966 from Bury, £60,000

LEFT: 1979, retired

CROWD IDOL RATING: * * * * *

NICKNAME: 'Nijinsky'

APPEARANCES: 498 (+3 as sub)

GOALS: 153

SPECIALITY: Non-stop running with a Rolls-Royce engine

SONG: 'We'll drink a drink a drink to Colin the King, the King, the King!'

UNLIKELY TO SAY: 'I must remember to send Martin Buchan a Christmas card'

GREAT GOAL: Stunning volley away to Chelsea, 1970

UNFORGETTABLE MOMENT: Returning from injury on Boxing Day 1977 v. Newcastle

FLAWS: None

Colin's tale: When Malcolm Allison sat in the stand at Gigg Lane loudly expressing his doubts over Colin Bell's ability, he was, of course, attempting to convince the other scouts that they were wasting their time watching the young Bury midfielder. 'He can't pass it,' he'd say absent-mindedly (but just loud enough for those sat nearby to hear). 'He can't tackle and he's no good in the air,' he'd continue. Whether anyone was fooled by this is unknown, but seeing as Allison managed to delay any other bids and snapped up Bell once City had the cash to buy him, it's just possible there were a couple of prospective buyers wondering why'd they'd ever been taken in by such an old ploy.

Wearing the No. 10 shirt rather than the No. 8 that he would later make his own, he made his debut in a 2–1 win at Derby and scored one of the goals. He played in all 11 remaining

Colin Bell, Francis Lee and Mike Summerbee – three top-notch Crowd Idols for the price of one and the on-field epicentre of the glory years

games, and City didn't lose a match, picking up the Division Two championship for good measure. His signing was already proving a resounding success weeks into his career.

Bell was an ever-present during his first full season and finished top scorer with a dozen goals as the Blues limped to a final placing of fifteenth in the table, but that was merely a warm-up for the incredible years ahead.

Francis Lee had joined the club midway through the 1967–68 season, and for many, this represented the final piece of the Mercer–Allison blueprint. City won the league title with Bell inspirational throughout the campaign. He was here, there and literally everywhere, and the fans loved his driving style and seemingly limitless stamina. He was the beating heart of the team and along with Lee and Mike Summerbee, formed the legendary 'Holy Trinity' of players who would inspire the club to, as yet, uncharted heights.

Bell also won his first England cap in 1968 – the first of 48, which is still a club record. He never scored winning goals in cup finals and rarely took the headlines for being anything other than brilliant. He was a fantastic footballer and a quiet man off the pitch, too, never seeking adulation or press coverage, even though he'd more than earned it. While Summerbee, Lee and Doyle would wind up the opposition, the press and opposing fans, Bell quietly ticked along in the background, painfully shy, preferring to let his feet do the talking – and how they talked!

He was to Manchester City what George Best was to Manchester United – the golden boy, the untouchable, the prodigal son. As the years ticked by, Bell's influence seemed to grow stronger rather than fade, and while the press and pundits claimed Rodney Marsh's signing cost City the 1971–72 league title, few noted that Colin Bell had missed nine games through injury, City winning just four of those matches.

Bell was fantastically loyal to City, and there was never the slightest suggestion that he would ever leave the club. Undoubtedly, every top club in Europe coveted the Blues' No. 8, but as the successful late '60s team slowly began to fragment, Bell powered on missing just three league games in three-and-a-half seasons.

Then came the infamous League Cup tie with Manchester United and the moment indelibly etched in the minds of all who witnessed it. Bell, attacking the Platt Lane end, was caught in two minds as to what to do as he approached Martin Buchan on the edge of the Reds' box. He opted to cut inside and was scythed down by the United man, effectively destroying his knee joint and, for all intents and purposes, ending his career.

He did come back later that season and was again on the end of a nasty challenge, this time from Ray Kennedy as the Blues beat Arsenal 3–1 at Maine Road – that injury was, many believed, equal to Buchan's challenge. He was sidelined for the next 18 months doing everything he possibly could to work his way back to fitness.

Quietly and stoically, he continued the long, painful road back to some kind of fitness, pounding the streets around Maine Road as some mobility returned before he was finally passed fit to begin training again. Of course, he made a comeback against Newcastle United as a second-half sub on Boxing Day 1977 and received the most emotional ovation ever witnessed at Maine Road, before or since. His appearance galvanised his teammates and the crowd, and City scored four goals to win the game. He played sporadically after that, but, understandably, he was never the same again. His bravery, though, was admired by all in football, and at City, the man was, and still is, a god. Finally, the pain and heartache of never being able to move fluidly on a pitch again forced his retirement.

It's unlikely City will ever have a player quite as complete as Colin Bell again.

NO. 2: THE GOAT – SHAUN GOATER

SIGNED: 1998 from Bristol City, £400,000

LEFT: 2003 for Reading, £500,000

CROWD IDOL RATING: * * * * *

NICKNAME: 'The Goat'

APPEARANCES: 189 (+ 23 as sub)

GOALS: 103

MOMENT IN TIME: His 100th City goal in the last-ever Manchester derby at Maine Road

SPECIALITY: Scoring off every bit of his anatomy and being in the right place at the right time on a regular basis

SONG: 'Feed the Goat and he will score, feed the Goat and he will score' and 'Who let the Goat out?'

NOT A LOT OF PEOPLE KNOW THAT: Goat's first name is Leonard

The Goat's story: Born and raised in Bermuda, Shaun Goater's career looked to be heading nowhere in particular. He was playing for island side North Village and apart from a future with the national team and their attempts to qualify for the World Cup, it was doubtful that he would have ever left his homeland to play football – few ever did.

But when a touring Manchester United stopped by for a midwinter break in 1988, Alex Ferguson offered the gangly teenager the opportunity of a life in England with one of the country's biggest clubs (yes, that did hurt). Goater left the paradise island and headed to the murky skies of northern England in search of fame and fortune.

Things didn't work out at United, and he never got a sniff of first-team football. With his contract nearly up, he was offered a chance at Rotherham United, and determined to earn a living in England, he took it. He stayed at Millmoor for seven years, banging in the goals and making a reputation for himself in the lower leagues, but there was little suggestion of what lay ahead for him. He scored 86 times in 209 starts for the Millers before Bristol City decided to take a punt on him.

Shaun Goater – fed on goals and
adored by the City fans

Now aged 26, the fee of £175,000 was the first cash anybody had ever spent on his services, but Bristol were soon pleased they had, as Goater bagged 45 goals in just 81 starts. That was when Joe Royle decided he needed a proven goalscorer to help his ailing side avoid relegation to Division Two.

At £400,000, the risk was small, and Royle also knew that if

City still went down in those final eight weeks of the season, he had a player in his side who knew the lower divisions and their demands very well. Goater scored three goals as the Blues failed to avoid the drop, and the jury was still very much out on the Bermudan.

As ever, the City fans decided to pack out Maine Road throughout the 1998–99 season in a bid to shout the team back to the top. Goater began to find the net regularly, but there were still doubts about his ability and whether he was the right man to lead the line. He played his part in promotion after controversially scoring the winner (some believed via his arm) in the play-off semi against Wigan and also gave his all in the play-off final against Gillingham, having a hand in the last-gasp Dickov equaliser. The seeds of affection had been officially sown.

City raced to promotion the next season, and Goater spearheaded the front-line with awkward grace that was difficult to pigeonhole. Some of his goals were stuffy, some were tap-ins and some were classy, but his name was on the score sheet in 23 games that year, and it was Goat's goal at Blackburn on the final day that sparked a dramatic turnaround from 0–1 down to 4–1 up and promotion to the Premiership.

With the terrace chant 'Feed the Goat and he will score' reverberating at Maine Road each time he played, Goater had, by now, become something of a talisman to the Blues' fans. In some ways, he embodied the club and its followers. He was honest, loyal, committed, and he'd had to make the best of what he had to succeed.

He only played a handful of games that season in the Premiership due to both injury and the fact that Royle had purchased George Weah and Paulo Wanchope. However, towards the final stages of the campaign, it was the more familiar forward line of Goater and occasionally Paul Dickov that led the attack, and despite missing half a season, Goat finished top scorer. He'd not only proved himself at the highest level after 11 years in England, he'd almost single-handedly saved City from the drop. Almost, but not quite.

Kevin Keegan took over as manager in the close season of 2001, and, again, many thought he'd bring in someone else to lead the line, but Keegan was cannier than that. He instead brought in a couple of midfielders who would create more chances for the strikers he'd inherited – and it worked like a charm.

Goater became the first City player in almost 30 years to score 30 league goals in a season, and in the eyes of his adoring fans, he could do no wrong. City were promoted at a canter and splashed out a record £13 million to bring in Nicolas Anelka. Once again, Shaun's days at Maine Road looked numbered.

It was also the last season at Maine Road, and, to many, it looked like the end of two wonderful eras was inevitable. When they played together, Goat and Anelka linked well, and for the final Manchester derby at Maine Road, the pair of strikers from opposite ends of the football spectrum combined to magical effect. Goat went into the game on 99 goals for City in all competitions, and if ever an afternoon was scripted, this was it.

With the score at 1–1, Gary Neville elected to shepherd a slow-moving ball out of play. Goat sniffed an opportunity, nicked it off him and at a tight angle made for goal. He looked up and coolly stroked it past Fabien Barthez to complete a century of goals for the Blues and very nearly lift the roof off Maine Road in the process. He then made it 101 shortly after half-time and sealed a famous 3–1 win. The ecstatic City fans left the ground chanting just one name, that of Shaun Goater.

In the return game, he scored the equaliser at Old Trafford after about ten seconds of arriving off the bench to secure a point for City – and that would be his last goal for the club. Keegan made it clear he didn't see many opportunities for Goat in the future and he played only the odd role here and there until the last day of the season, when Keegan fittingly made him captain for his last Maine Road match ever.

The reception Shaun Goater received that day showed the love the City fans had for a player who overcame all the odds and also completely won over the many supporters who felt he wasn't up to the task. It was an emotional day but also a deserved and – apart from the result – fitting tribute to one of the most popular players – and men – to have ever played for Manchester City FC.

Crowd Idols don't come much bigger than this.

NO. 1: THE GEORGIAN MAESTRO –

GEORGI KINKLADZE

SIGNED: 1995 from Dinamo Tbilisi, £2 million

LEFT: 1998 for Ajax, £5.5 million

CROWD IDOL RATING: * * * * *

NICKNAME: 'Kinky'

APPEARANCES: 120 (+1 as sub)

GOALS: 22

MOMENT IN TIME: His solo goal against Southampton in March 1996

SPECIALITY: You name it – he had it. Vision and dribbling ability would be near the top, though

NOT A LOT OF PEOPLE KNOW THAT: Gio once played for Argentinian side Boca Juniors and his hero was Diego Maradona

Kinky's story: City had signed a number of nobodies from abroad, so when Georgi Kinkladze signed from Dinamo Tbilisi during the summer of 1995, it caused little attention in the national media. At £2 million it seemed like a bit of a gamble considering City's dire financial plight, but the deal was brokered and backed by chairman Francis Lee, who, having watched several videos of Kinkladze in action, was determined to bring the Georgian midfielder to Manchester.

Kinky, as he was soon to become better known, had starred for Dinamo for several years, but at 22, the club knew they had to cash in on him sooner or later. Besides, the unstable political situation in Georgia meant it was safer to move abroad and earn a living rather than be a potential kidnap victim or worse. He had been shipped out on loan to Boca Juniors and German side Saarbrücken, had trained with Real Madrid and been courted by AC Milan and Juventus. Barcelona were also said to be monitoring his progress, but it was City who made the first move, largely on the basis of Kinky's display as Georgia beat Wales 1–0 in Cardiff during a European Championship qualifier. In that game, Colin Bell and Tony Book sat and watched the talented youngster dictate the game and score the only goal, a superb chip from 20 yards that Neville Southall didn't bother moving for.

The message to chairman Lee was clear – sign Kinkladze at all costs. Lee moved quickly and set up a deal that ensured the player would be in a sky-blue shirt come August. Kinky made his debut against Spurs and showed vision and breathtaking touches that the City fans, to be quite honest, just weren't used to. But the team was in rapid decline, and it wouldn't be until November that the first Premiership victory was recorded. Kinky must have wondered if he'd chosen the right club!

There were some dark days that season, but the one thing that kept the supporters going was Kinky and his magical box of tricks. He scored his first goal against Aston Villa after playing a lovely one-two with Niall Quinn, and a fortnight later, he faced Brazilian star Juninho at Middlesbrough in a contest that was billed as a battle of two breathtaking individual talents. Kinky, quite simply, was in another league and scored a fantastic solo goal, even though it was in vain as the Blues lost 4–1.

Alan Ball had a terrible time as City boss, but the one thing he did get right was how best to handle Kinkladze – it was just the other ten he had problems with! By Christmas, it is fair to say that the City fans were in complete awe of the most technically gifted player ever to represent the club.

Against Southampton he scored the goal of a lifetime, beating at least five players before coolly chipping Dave Beasant. At the end of the season, Tony Yeboah's volley for Leeds United at Wimbledon took the Goal of the Season award on *Match of*

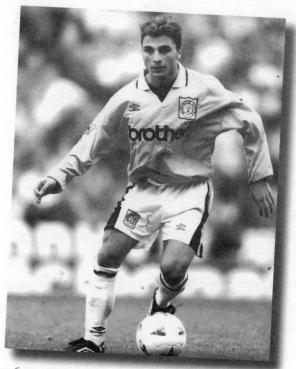

Georgi Kinkladze – an incredibly gifted talent

the Day – what a load of utter crap. If Kinky had been wearing a Manchester United shirt, he would have walked off with the award and it would still be regularly replayed even today.

It is hard to describe in words the pride Georgi gave to City fans during that desperate season. He was the one shining light amid a sea of mediocrity and gloom and when the club finally lost its battle against relegation on the final day of the campaign, Kinky cried – and many believed that was that. Why should he stay? There were bigger and more prestigious platforms to play on than the one City were giving him.

Franny Lee, however, somehow convinced the 23-year-old genius to remain a Blue rather than join any number of interested suitors in the Premiership, Serie A or La Liga.

What the conversation must have been like, God only knows, but quite how Lee sold him on the idea of Southend and Tranmere instead of Inter or AC is perhaps more testament to Franny's persuasiveness than actual fact. He did stay, and short of carrying a neon sign on the pitch saying 'Stop me and win one', he soon paid the price. He became an easy target for the Division One bully boys, and teams would put two, sometimes three players on him in order to stop City's one productive outlet. Left alone, he would destroy any club in that division, but hacked, battered and hassled, he would either limp off or try and get rid of the ball as quickly as possible so as not to lose a limb. It really was that bad, and it was painful to watch for his many fans. For some of the lows – a 4–1 defeat at Lincoln City, for instance – he was spared the pain and rested, but he was back for the second leg, and he couldn't stop another defeat. He must have been thinking, 'Why the hell did I stay?' And why not – everybody else was. Sometimes it showed on his face, but he soldiered on, dreaming of better times.

It was hardly doing his career any good and who knew whether the next lunge might injure him permanently? It seemed a matter of when he would leave rather than if, and City fans, well aware that if he went, the club were up the proverbial creek, organised a Kinkladze day for the final match against Reading to show their collective appreciation. He was actually injured for the game but a full house shouted his name from start to finish and waved Georgian flags in the vain hope of convincing him to stay. The reception at the end when he appeared with the rest of the squad was monumental, and if he had been planning to move, it seems this was enough to change his mind.

With people camped outside his Wilmslow home, he asked his sister, 'How can I leave these people when there is so much love?' How indeed? In an ill-fated but amazingly loyal gesture he decided to stay and give it one final push. The tackles got worse, and his form and whole demeanour suggested he was incredibly unhappy. It brought to memory the Oscar Wilde story about the swallow that is set to fly away to warm sunny climes but befriends a gold-encrusted statue who convinces the bird to stay in order to bring happiness to others. In the story, the little bird dies after continually putting off its migration and though nothing so dramatic happened here, staying one more year was pretty much the death of Kinky's chance to play for a top European club.

It soon became clear that City weren't going to go up and were in fact headed the other way. Joe Royle was appointed midway through the campaign, after the City fans had endured a succession of useless managers, and his first decision was to sell Kinky, who he felt there was 'an unhealthy obsession' with at the club. In some ways he was right – the time had come to part company. Gio knew it and so did the fans. He eventually agreed to join Ajax, and though Royle dropped him for much of the season run-in, Kinky desperately wanted to play. Many believe that if he had played, relegation would have been avoided, but, alas, we'll never know for sure.

He flew back from an international game for Georgia to sit on the bench in the final match of the season. City needed to win and others to lose. Of course, we were relegated. Kinky came on for the final few minutes to a wonderful ovation but even he was powerless to stop City falling into the nation's third tier for the first time in the club's history. He looked as crestfallen as he did in his first season with the club and applauded the fans with tears streaming down his face. He threw his boots into the crowd and walked down the tunnel for the last time.

Colin Bell may well be the club's favourite son, but Georgi Kinkladze was probably *the* Crowd Idol of all time, based on raw passion, hero worship and unwithheld admiration, including that of this writer – if you hadn't already guessed!

EXTRA TIME

So that's it – did you agree with the Top 50 or would yours be completely different? I'm sure there'll be a number of readers who disagree with the top ten positioning, but I've never witnessed such an outpouring of emotion to one player as that afforded to Georgi Kinkladze. There is no doubt that Colin Bell is the club's greatest ever player, and he was definitely an idol, too, but I don't think anyone has matched the near hysteria that followed Kinky around during his first two seasons with City.

Shaun Goater also finished ahead of King Colin, but that's because this book is about Crowd Idols – not legends or heroes. We've all seen a dozen books like that, and I didn't want an obvious end to this one. Many of these players would never have appeared in those oft-published tomes – and there's the real crime, because they have each played their part over the last 40 years and deserve some kind of recognition.

If you agree, I'm glad; if you don't, I understand. Everyone has his or her own ideas of an idol and that's what makes football the greatest game on the planet – and puts the Blues and their supporters in a league of their own.